PAUL

PAUL

A very brief history

JOHN M. G. BARCLAY

First published in Great Britain in 2017

Society for Promoting Christian Knowledge
36 Causton Street
London SW1P 4ST
www.spck.org.uk

British Library Cataloguing-in-Publication Data
A catalogue record for this book is available from the British Library

ISBN 978–0–281–07607–9
eBook ISBN 978–0–281–07608–6

Typeset by Manila Typesetting Company
First printed in Great Britain by Ashford Colour Press
Subsequently digitally printed in Great Britain

eBook by Manila Typesetting Company

Produced on paper from sustainable forests

For Morna Hooker,
an inspiration to all her students

Contents

Chronology   xii

Part 1
THE HISTORY

1 Paul in the early Christian movement   3

2 Paul's letters and their historical situations   13

3 Paul and the Jewish tradition   23

4 Paul's churches in the Roman world   30

5 Early images of Paul   38

Part 2
THE LEGACY

6 Paul as Scripture   49

7 Augustine and the Western Church   56

8 Paul in the Protestant tradition   64

9 Paul in Jewish–Christian relations   72

10 Paul as social and cultural critic   79

Further reading   88

Index   89

Chronology

All dates Common Era (CE) = AD.

?–*c.*30	Jesus
*c.*10–*c.*62	Paul
312	Conversion of Constantine
354–430	Augustine of Hippo
1225–74	Thomas Aquinas
1483–1546	Martin Luther
1509–64	John Calvin
From late eighteenth century	Modern critical scholarship on Paul

Part 1

THE HISTORY

1

Paul in the early Christian movement

Paul was a Jewish intellectual, a travelling craftsman, and a propagandist for a set of new and extraordinary claims about Jesus of Nazareth. He first vigorously opposed the Jesus movement, but then energetically pioneered its spread beyond its Jewish homeland, focusing on the recruitment of non-Jews ('the nations'; 'the Gentiles'). He founded and then fostered a network of churches ('assemblies') in cities around the north of the Mediterranean, from Syria to Italy, restlessly travelling and writing letters in order to promote what he considered a last-generation effort to save a doomed world. He fell out with some of the churches he founded, scandalized more cautious members of the Jesus movement, was opposed by many of his fellow Jews, and eventually fell foul of the Roman authorities. As a result, many of his mission plans were never fulfilled and his life was prematurely ended by his execution in Rome. But by that time what became known as the 'Christian' movement had become sufficiently robust to survive, and its growth and cross-cultural adaptability were greatly aided by Paul's insistence that non-Jewish 'believers' were not required to adopt core Jewish practices. Moreover, Paul was as versatile in thought as in practice, and in his surviving letters he left a legacy of subtle and fertile theology that has wielded ever since an enormous influence on Christian thought and Western culture.

Such was Paul's impact, and so many and varied were the early Christian claims to his legacy, that many 'Pauls' were soon generated and many legends recounted, some more flattering than others. A historian wishing to reconstruct the 'original Paul' needs to weigh the sources carefully. The general rules of history apply: the earlier the source the better; primary sources (from Paul himself) are more important than secondary sources (texts written by others about him); and all of our sources have their own 'slant' – none is entirely unbiased (and neither are we). There is no surviving trace of Paul in contemporary sources from outside the Christian movement, but of the Christian sources the earliest and most important are his own letters and the admiring portrayal of his mission in the Acts of the Apostles (Acts for short), which was probably written some 20–30 years after Paul's death (i.e. 80s–90s CE). Acts gives its account of the early Church in the mode of ancient historiography: it mixes traditions of various sources and kinds, and shapes them rhetorically to form a gripping narrative. We shall return to Acts below, among the 'Early images of Paul' (Chapter 5), but here we note that for a historian it carries less weight than letters written by Paul himself.

But which letters come from Paul? We may discount the later and obviously fictitious correspondence between Paul and Seneca, or the made-up letter known as 3 Corinthians. By the middle of the second century there were 13 letters attributed to Paul, the 13 that bear his name in the New Testament. (Later, the treatise included in the New Testament under the title 'Hebrews' was also sometimes attributed to Paul, but it is anonymous, and the product of another, equally creative, mind.) For most of Christian history, and for most Christians today, all 13 letters are regarded as equally 'Pauline', but in the modern era of historical criticism (i.e. since the eighteenth century), all ancient texts, including these letters, have been subject to critical questions about their authorship and origin. We shall explore in the next chapter how modern scholars distinguish between 'authentic' and 'inauthentic' (or 'deutero-Pauline') letters, but we may note for now that, for most contemporary historians, we hear Paul's authentic voice only in seven of the letters bearing his name: 1 Thessalonians, 1 Corinthians, 2 Corinthians, Galatians, Philemon, Philippians and Romans. These, then, are the main primary sources that we will use at this point for our historical reconstruction of Paul's life and thought.

After the death of Jesus (in the early 30s CE), some of his disciples announced that God had raised him from the dead, recounting experiences of the risen Jesus that made them reframe everything they had previously thought about Jesus and about their Jewish Scriptures and traditions. The energy of this group, and their momentous claims about Jesus as the Jewish Messiah (Christ) and the Lord of the world, caused controversy among Jews in Jerusalem. But when Jewish believers spread this message in the synagogues of neighbouring cities, a whole new layer of controversy arose. Within or on the edges of these Jewish communities were non-Jewish sympathizers (sometimes called 'God-fearers') who respected the Jewish community and its tradition, but did not make the full commitment to the Jewish Law necessary to become converts to Judaism (for men, that entailed circumcision). It appears that the Jesus message proved attractive in such circles. It spoke of salvation given by the one true God through trust in what he had done in the life, death and resurrection of the 'Lord Jesus'; it promised entry into the people of God and the hope of salvation through a simple rite of washing ('baptism'); and it demonstrated the presence of the risen Jesus in miracles and in other new experiences of the power of God understood as the work of his Spirit.

This is where Paul comes into the picture, in the mid 30s CE. According to his own testimony, Paul was actively seeking to 'destroy' the Jesus movement in or around Damascus, out of zeal for his ancestral Jewish traditions (Galatians 1.13–14; Philippians 3.5–6). He probably came from Tarsus, in the province of Cilicia (south-east Turkey), born of Jewish parents ('a Hebrew born of Hebrews'), and given a Jewish education, through which he acquired an encyclopedic knowledge of the Jewish Scriptures in their Greek translation. It is possible that part of this education was in Jerusalem (as claimed in Acts 22.3), but Paul seems thoroughly at home in the Diaspora (outside the Jewish homeland), where there were large and well-established communities of Hellenistic Jews (e.g. in Alexandria, Antioch and Damascus). Paul describes himself as a Pharisee (Philippians 3.5), a movement among Jews renowned for the precision with which they interpreted the Torah (the Jewish Law). Something about the Jesus movement outraged Paul when he encountered it in Damascus. Perhaps it was its shocking claims about Jesus, whose crucifixion by the Romans marked him as a failed and now insignificant rebel. Or perhaps it was the way the Jesus movement attracted non-Jews and treated them as full members of God's people on terms that seemed contrary to the Torah and to everything that Paul valued in his ancestral tradition.

Thus when Paul first encountered the Jesus movement he was its deadly opponent. He had not met Jesus, but he was convinced that his opposition to this movement was the proper expression of his loyalty to God. What happened next was not the resolution of an inner psychological tension, nor the salving of a guilty conscience, but a revolution in his understanding of the world, of himself, of right and wrong, and of the God he worshipped. What he experienced at or near Damascus was, he says, a 'revelation', in which he was granted a vision of the risen Jesus (Galatians 1.15–16; 1 Corinthians 15.8–10). He was now convinced that Jesus was indeed 'Lord', the agent through whom God would rule the world, and that in Jesus' death and resurrection God had begun to save the world. In this, the original 'Damascus-road experience', Paul underwent a fundamental reorientation of his life and loyalties.

We cannot now trace all the shifts that took place in Paul's mind immediately after this revelation, since the first of his surviving letters (1 Thessalonians) dates from more than ten years later. But as Paul would later describe it, what happened in this event was a 'calling' effected by the grace of God (Galatians 1.15; 1 Corinthians 15.10). His description echoes the commissioning of 'the servant' in Isaiah (Isaiah 49.1–6), whose mission embraced 'the nations' just as Paul's calling impelled him to preach the good news among non-Jews (Galatians 1.16). But 'calling' in Paul means more than commission: it is the word he uses for what we term 'conversion' (1 Corinthians 1.26; 7.17–24; Galatians 1.6); that is, the start of a new relation to God. Paul did not 'convert' in the sense of 'changing religion' (a modern way of putting things), since the God who 'called' him was the same God he had always tried to serve. But this event revolutionized his understanding of his own tradition, because he now regarded Jesus as the centre and fulfilment of all God's purposes, and in rereading his Scriptures he found there numerous echoes of this good news. And it revolutionized his moral and theological coordinates. If his persecution of the Church, which he had thought 100 per cent right, was in fact 100 per cent wrong, and if God revealed Christ and called Paul *despite* such a fundamental sin, it was clear that God's grace was not given on the basis of human worth. That was an unnerving discovery, since it was normally (and understandably) imagined that God's best gifts were differentially distributed according to the worth of the recipients. But if God's favour was given *without respect for worth*, it was not limited, Paul came to see, by any ethnic criteria. It could be experienced even by non-Jews, whom Paul had considered out-and-out 'sinners' because of their 'idolatry' and shameful moral practices. God's gift to the *unworthy* paralleled and was based upon the death and resurrection of Christ, since God had raised the crucified Jesus – in human terms worthless, and in Jewish terms 'cursed' (Galatians 3.13). Although Paul shows rather little interest in recycling the teaching of Jesus, his thought revolves around the great reversal that took place in the crucifixion and resurrection of Jesus, and that took place likewise in him. As he puts it in Galatians, 'I have been crucified with Christ: it is no longer I who live but Christ who lives in me' (Galatians 2.19–20).

After Paul's Damascus experience we can trace some of his geographical movements, though it is impossible to determine a precise chronology. Paul narrates only fragments of his story, and it is unclear how much we can rely on the narrative in Acts which, where it overlaps with Paul, does not always cohere with his account of his life. Paul teamed up first with Barnabas, founding communities of believers in and around Antioch (in Syria), perhaps partly in and partly outside the parameters of Jewish synagogue communities. Their work was controversial when it became known among more traditional members of the Jerusalem church (for reasons we shall trace in Chapter 3), but at a conference in Jerusalem a compromise allowed them to continue enlisting non-Jewish members without requiring males to get circumcised (Galatians 2.1–10). But the compromise did not hold. A dispute arose at Antioch at which Paul's conduct of the mission to non-Jews was criticized, and he found himself in a heated argument with Peter (Galatians 2.11–14). Thereafter he probably lost his support base in Antioch and moved progressively west, accompanied by other colleagues (Titus, Timothy and Silvanus/ Silas), through the provinces of Galatia and Asia (central and west Turkey), and then over to Macedonia and Greece. As he travelled, he spread his good news about Jesus, sometimes in Jewish synagogues and sometimes in the workshops where he plied his (leather-working?) trade, talking in vivid and urgent terms to customers and fellow workers. Little clusters of believers were formed in cities in Galatia, in Colossae and Ephesus, in Thessalonica, Philippi and Corinth, and in other urban centres, some vividly portrayed in Paul's surviving letters, some now lost from memory. Such churches met in homes or shops, most, perhaps, with fewer than 30 members.

Paul was a restless missionary, not least because he expected that Jesus would return and wrap up history within his lifetime (1 Thessalonians 4.13–18). Most of his converts were from a non-Jewish background, and he began to worry that the Jesus movement would split along ethnic

lines between Jerusalem-organized groups of Jewish believers and his own network of churches, who were not only
ethnically different but also more socially adapted to the
Hellenized world of the eastern Roman Empire. He con-
ceived the idea of raising a significant sum of money from
his churches and taking it to Jerusalem as poor relief, a gift
that (like all ancient gifts) would create social ties and thus
keep the movement together. It proved a lot harder than he
expected to raise the money – not least because his most
successful church, in Corinth, withdrew their trust in him.
But eventually, by the mid 50s CE, he had gathered a suitable
collection. He wanted to press his mission further west to
Rome, and from Rome to Spain, but he decided first to ac-
company the money to Jerusalem, while nervous about his
reception there (Romans 15.14–33).

It was a fateful decision. According to Acts, Paul was
treated with suspicion, even downright hostility, by the
Jerusalem church, and it is likely that they refused to accept
the collection. In any case, he was arrested in Jerusalem
by Roman authorities and charged with causing unrest.
He had been in prison elsewhere on previous occasions
for short periods, but this time the proceedings dragged
on. After years in prison in Caesarea, he was sent to Rome
under armed escort, so that his case could be heard in an
imperial court. Earlier, when he was setting off with the
collection to Jerusalem, Paul had written in friendly terms
to the believers in Rome to introduce his mission and his
message, but they had never met him in person, and they
too, it seems, were wary of him. We do not know what happened after Paul's arrival in Rome (Acts becomes vague and
breaks off at this point), but he may have been ensnared
in the growing suspicion of Christians that justified Nero's

campaign against them after the fire in Rome in 64 CE. In fact, his trial may have made clear to the Roman authorities that the Jesus movement was not welcome in the Jewish community, and thus should not benefit from the privileges and exemptions accorded to Jews. Paul was probably executed, in the early 60s, on a charge of sedition or of disturbing the peace. He was perhaps in his early fifties.

For 30 years Paul had played a major role in the development of the Jesus movement. This was its first, formative generation, a time of expansion, cultural transition and internal controversy, and Paul was deeply involved in all those dynamics. It is hard to assess his comparative importance. Although he presents himself as uniquely called as 'apostle to the nations', there were others who carried the 'good news' around the Roman world: when he wrote to the believers in Rome he had to introduce himself somewhat awkwardly as their apostle, although he had not founded any of their house-churches. Even in his own churches other figures wielded considerable authority, some of whom he tolerated (Apollos in Corinth), while others he regarded as deadly enemies, even servants of Satan (2 Corinthians 11.15). But although he was not the only apostle spreading the message of Jesus in the non-Jewish world, Paul probably had the widest influence and the biggest reputation (both positive and negative). Most importantly, he gave to the early Christian movement a clear Jewish (i.e. scriptural) rationale for its spread into the non-Jewish world, and for its mission among non-Jews on terms that integrated them as full members of God's people ('children of Abraham') without requiring them to live like Jews. Thus, at this foundational stage, he played a critical role in enabling the Jesus movement to cross the cultural boundary between Judaism and the non-Jewish world without losing its identity as the fulfilment of God's purposes for Israel. Without Paul's energy and influence, the Jesus movement might have remained only a controversial and ultimately unsuccessful sect within Judaism, unable to communicate or to recruit in the non-Jewish world. Or it could have become a worldwide Jesus cult wholly alienated from its Jewish heritage. The creative thought and the restless action of Paul ensured that the mainstream Christian movement took neither of these routes. Instead it inducted non-Jewish believers into a movement that retained its Jewish ideological and textual roots but was capable of finding social and cultural expression among Greeks, Syrians, Cretans, Egyptians and Romans, and eventually in almost every culture across the globe.

2

Paul's letters and their historical situations

Paul's letters are all that remains of Paul – notwithstanding some claims to possess various parts of his skeleton. But we are extraordinarily fortunate to possess this literary legacy. Through these letters we get direct access to Paul's mind and personality – in fact, fuller and more immediate access than for anyone else in the early Jesus movement. Moreover, because they respond to diverse situations in his churches, they are by far our most precious source for the challenges that faced the very first generation of (what came to be called) Christianity. And because Paul responds to these challenges from his newly minted theological perspective, his letters evidence some of the most creative thinking in early Christianity – thinking that, together with John's Gospel, has formed the chief foundation for most subsequent Christian theology.

It is important to emphasize that Paul wrote *letters*, not theological treatises. In other words, none of these letters contains a compendium of Paul's thought, systematically arranged. Even the letter that comes closest to such a description – the letter to the Romans – contains only parts of Paul's thought, and is shaped by the situation in which it was written and to which it was addressed. In reading Paul's letters, we are reading other people's mail:

Paul's mind was directed to one place at one time, not to posterity, nor even to a wide contemporary audience. For a historian, that makes them all the more fascinating, especially where we can trace developments over time, as in the relationship between Paul and the church in Corinth. But the individuality of each letter inevitably makes identifying 'Paul's view' on anything a complicated matter. Even when taken individually, the letters are quite complex and even ambiguous documents; when they were collected, circulated and (eventually) canonized, the differences between them added a further layer of complexity to their interpretation. For not only does Paul address different topics; he sometimes addresses the same topics (e.g. the Jewish Law) in different ways and from different perspectives. That is what you would expect in varied correspondence written to different destinations over a period of time. As the historian has to remind the theologian, Paul was a situational thinker: he was undoubtedly engaged in doing theology, but he was more a practical than a systematic theologian.

Paul's letters are the residue of his mission and of the networks that emerged as he laid mission plans, planted new churches, and anxiously watched their development. Most are addressed to churches he had founded (Romans is the exception), answering their questions or complaints, attacking opponents, and encouraging, warning or instructing his converts. They are among the most vivid correspondence we possess from the ancient world, rich in personal detail, as news flew around Paul's networks through messengers and delegates. That news was generally conveyed to Paul orally (e.g. by members of Chloe's household, 1 Corinthians 1.11), though we also know of a letter written to Paul, from the church in Corinth (1 Corinthians 7.1).

When Paul wrote back (normally with the aid of a scribe, Romans 16.22), he used trusted agents to carry his letters and to reinforce his message when they read his letters aloud (e.g. Phoebe, Romans 16.1–2). Thus Paul's letters are a substitute for his presence, and they attempt to convey his authority from a distance. Sometimes that authority was questioned, either by members of his own churches (e.g. in Corinth) or by other 'apostles' (missionaries) who supplemented or countered Paul's message (e.g. in Corinth and in Galatia). In the letter to the Romans, Paul was writing ahead to a cluster of churches whose support he needed for his mission in Spain. But here and elsewhere intervention by letter was a delicate matter. Not everyone was delighted to receive a letter from Paul, and not everyone agreed with what he wrote.

Paul wrote many more letters than those that have survived (see 1 Corinthians 5.9), and it is not clear why some were preserved and others were not. One might have expected some of the surviving letters to have disappeared (e.g. his exceptionally rude letter to the churches in Galatia), and it is a mystery why the highly specific appeal for the slave Onesimus (the letter to Philemon) survived alongside the larger and more multifaceted letters. The fact that Paul's letters were later collected (we don't know when or by whom) suggests that they attracted interest and were accorded wide authority after his death. And since it was clear that Paul's thought was constantly in motion, it was natural to ask what he would have said in new situations that arose when he was no longer available to address them.

One way of answering that question was to quote his letters or to reuse his language in addressing new crises, as in the letters of Clement of Rome and Ignatius of Antioch (at the end of the first century and beginning of the second). Another, it seems, was to compose new letters in his name, applying, developing and reshaping his thoughts for new contexts. Most modern historians have come to conclude that several of the letters in the New Testament that bear Paul's name fall into this latter category – letters written out of respect for Paul, and to continue his legacy, but by someone else, and after his lifetime. The same, they think, is true with regard to Peter, James and Jude, because this phenomenon (called pseudepigraphy) was common in the ancient world, not least among Jews of this time. But our focus here is specifically on Paul.

All historical judgements are contestable and, understandably, judgements about the authorship of the Pauline letters have been heavily contested over the last 200 years of scholarly enquiry. But the historians' hypotheses go something like this. Someone who loved Paul's letters, and wanted to apply Paul's thought to a new crisis in the Church, wrote a letter in his name, perhaps not long after his death, to a fictional setting in Colossae (the letter called Colossians). That letter was so profound in its development of Paul's thought that it inspired another author to write a mini-compendium of Pauline theology in the form of a general letter (originally without an explicit addressee, but now known as Ephesians). At about the same time, or perhaps a little later, another 'Paulinist' was inspired by 1 Thessalonians to write an updated imitation, known as 2 Thessalonians. And rather later than all these, when many groups were claiming Paul's authority for incompatible versions of Christian truth, new letters were created in Paul's name, one addressed to Timothy (1 Timothy) and one to Titus. Each has Paul speak in strong terms against anonymous teachers who 'pervert' the truth, while urging the appointment of reliable leaders who will continue the 'healthy' tradition. Another letter, written in a similar style, but as Paul's 'last will and testament', has the apostle pass on his mantle to his 'beloved child', Timothy (2 Timothy). (Taken together, these last three, 1 and 2 Timothy and Titus, are known as 'the Pastoral Epistles', and possibly date from the early second century.)

How do historians make judgements like these? In principle, on exactly the same grounds as one decides the authorship of any document, whether ancient treatises wrongly attributed to Aristotle, or modern sensations like the purported diaries of Hitler. The three main grounds are:

- where the *style* seems significantly different from that of the letters we know are by Paul – in sentence construction, in patterns of vocabulary, or in the use of sentence-connecting words called 'particles' (for obvious reasons, only those who know Greek very well can offer a reliable judgement here);
- where the *historical context* addressed by these letters seems to reflect a time *after* or *other than* Paul's own context (e.g. the controversies and patterns of church life found in the Pastoral Epistles); and
- where the *theological content* seems markedly different from what we know of the historical Paul, too different to be simply a further turn of his flexible mind.

If the current consensus among historians is right, six of the letters attributed to Paul in the New Testament are 'inauthentic' or 'deutero-Pauline'. They would represent, then, the first stages in the history of interpretation of Paul. Like the interest on an original deposit that has since been absorbed into the capital, they have generally been treated without distinction as belonging to Paul himself. Indeed, through most of Christian history – and in most church contexts today – all 13 letters in the New Testament carrying Paul's name function equally as the letters of Paul. A modern historian, in writing the history of Paul, would distinguish between 'the letters of the historical Paul' (Romans; 1 and 2 Corinthians; Galatians; 1 Thessalonians; Philippians; Philemon) and 'the letters of Paul influential through history' (all 13 letters in the New Testament that are attributed to Paul). For even if the disputed letters are not, in fact, by Paul, they have been successfully embedded into the tradition that goes under his name such that, outside of academic and academic-influenced circles in the last 200 years, they effectively count as Paul's own letters.

For now, however, we will stick with the historical Paul and focus on the seven generally 'undisputed' letters, briefly sketching their contexts and contents. We will take them in what may be the order in which they were written, although there are too many uncertainties about the chronology of Paul's life to be able to determine confidently the sequence of these letters.

1 Thessalonians was written to the church that Paul had just founded in the city of Thessalonica (now in northern Greece). He was clearly worried about these believers because of the social and economic hardship they had experienced since they had, as he puts it, 'turned to God from idols, to serve the living and true God' (1 Thessalonians 1.9). That break with their ancestral tradition, and thus with their family and civic religion, was bound to be socially offensive, and Paul fears lest they buckle under pressure. They have also experienced the death of one or more

of their members, and Paul has to assure them that the deceased will not miss out on the arrival of Jesus, which he clearly expected soon. Thus the letter is full of assurances, while it paints the world in dualistic terms: the children of light who are called by God will soon be vindicated, whereas 'sudden destruction' will come on everyone else.

1 Corinthians was written in response to news that Paul had received from Corinth (southern Greece). The church there was successful and its leaders socially and culturally at ease in their civic environment – in fact, more at ease than Paul liked. His letter challenges them on a variety of fronts: for their fascination with rhetoric and its social values ('wisdom'); for their division into factions around personalities; for their tolerance of a man who was living with his stepmother; for their lax attitude to eating food that had been offered in their presence to pagan deities ('idols'); for their insensitive conduct at the Lord's Supper towards those who were relatively poor; for their excessive fascination with speaking in tongues; and for their difficulty in believing in resurrection, in the sense of a future resurrected body (as opposed to the continuation of a disembodied soul). The range of theological and pastoral issues here addressed has made this letter perennially attractive to preachers.

2 Corinthians reflects the next and highly complex phase in Paul's relationship to the church in Corinth, after some had challenged his authority and criticized him for his physical weakness. (Some scholars think that 2 Corinthians is actually a compilation of up to five different letters written to Corinth over a short spell of time.) To deal with this crisis, Paul here deploys a remarkable set of theological and rhetorical resources. He redefines his apostolic role, cajoles and comforts the Corinthian believers, and boasts

ironically in his weakness (including his famous 'thorn in the flesh') in order to direct attention away from himself and to make the Corinthians rethink what they mean by 'weakness' and 'strength'. Here Paul's emotions (sorrow and joy, anger and love) can be witnessed at their most raw, as he wrestles theologically with profound questions concerning suffering.

Galatians is Paul's angriest letter, as he responds to news that the gospel he preached in Galatia (central Turkey) is being supplemented (in his view, destroyed) by other missionaries who are demanding that male believers get circumcised in order to become proper converts. In an argument full of citations from the Jewish Scriptures, Paul insists that this demand is not only unnecessary but disastrous: it would undermine what had been achieved by Christ, which was a gift unconditioned by the ethnic or cultural worth of its recipients. To compel non-Jews to 'Judaize' would be, Paul insists, to undo the freedom they have been granted by Christ, a freedom to walk by the Spirit, not regulated by the Law of Moses. The highly polemical tone of this letter, and its antithetical structures of thought, have made it a manifesto for radical interpretations of Paul.

Philemon was written to the church that met in the house of Philemon (we don't know where); it concerns a household slave, Onesimus, who has come to Paul to request his intervention in a domestic dispute. While with Paul, Onesimus has become a believer, and Paul, in sending him back, tactfully represents him as truly 'useful' (the meaning of his name), indeed a 'brother' and 'more than a slave'. The letter is so delicately phrased that it is hard to know exactly what Paul is requesting, but it gives us a fascinating glimpse into the way Paul does theology in difficult personal situations.

Philippians was written to the church in Philippi (northern Greece), with which Paul had, to all appearances, a very good relationship. Paul is writing from prison somewhere, and he encourages them to stick with him, despite his social and political shame. He also reinforces the counter-cultural values of the Christian movement, offering a pithy narrative of the humility and exaltation of Christ (the 'Christ-hymn', Philippians 2.6–11) that remains one of the most influential statements of Christian theology. Paul takes the financial support that he has received from this church as a sign of their shared dependence on the grace of God.

Finally, Romans, the longest of the letters, introduces Paul and his gospel to the churches in Rome, in preparation for his planned visit (on his way, he hoped, to Spain). Many themes from earlier letters are here taken up and reshaped into a large-scale narrative of salvation. The opening four chapters focus on the human condition of sin, and on God's gracious act of justification in Christ. In the clash of cosmic powers, where Grace overcomes the power of Sin and Death, rescue has come through the death and resurrection of Christ, appropriated through baptism and via the inner work of the Spirit (chapters 5—8). Three chapters (9—11) on God's merciful purposes for Israel place the event of Christ on a large historical map, and the final chapters (12—16) apply the principles of Paul's ethics to the churches in Rome, while announcing Paul's plans for his journeys first to Jerusalem and then to Rome.

The length and depth of the letter to the Romans has made it the centrepiece for most summaries of Paul's theology, and the influence of this one letter on the history of Christian thought has been simply enormous. But all these letters have found deep resonance through history (the letter to Philemon is the partial exception), as we shall trace in Part 2. Even from this outline it should be clear that these letters are varied and engaging. Unravelling Paul's thought and tracing his logic have been tasks big enough to challenge some of the greatest theological intellects. Those with more historical interests have found plenty of clues for the investigation of the earliest stages of the Christian movement. But there is also something deeply personal and engaging about these letters, and even those who dislike aspects of Paul's character cannot help but be drawn to these letters by his passionate and highly individual style. We meet here, in fact, one of the most interesting and unusual characters from the ancient world.

3

Paul and the Jewish tradition

Paul identifies himself as a Jew (Galatians 2.15) and an Israelite (Romans 11.1), with strong emotional bonds to his Jewish 'kin', even when they were yet to believe in Christ (Romans 9.1–5). His theology is rooted in the Jewish tradition in myriad ways, most obviously by drawing on many levels from the Jewish Scriptures. The Greek translations of the Scriptures were the Bible for Jews who lived, like Paul, in the Mediterranean Diaspora, and it is likely that Paul had a Greek-medium Jewish education in which he memorized many of those texts. But the Scriptures were more than a fund of vocabulary and a source of handy citations; their larger narrative structures and their deep theological thematics provided the framework in which Paul thought. When he reflects on the human condition, he talks of Adam, drawing from the opening chapters of Genesis (1 Corinthians 15; Romans 5). When he considers how God calls and shapes his people, he goes to the founding figure of Abraham (Galatians 3; Romans 4). The scriptural acclamation of the oneness of God (Deuteronomy 6.4) is central to Paul's theology (e.g. Romans 3.30), and he takes for granted its corresponding condemnation of the worship of false 'gods' or 'idols' (Romans 1). When he warns his Corinthian converts against dabbling with 'idolatry' he rehearses the stories (from Exodus and Numbers) of 'our fathers' in the desert (1 Corinthians 10). He even finds his own mission predicted by the scriptural tradition, especially in the Genesis promises that Abraham would be 'the father of many nations' (Galatians 3; Romans 4). In fact, Paul regards his non-Jewish converts not as replacing but as joining Israel in their common dependence on the mercy of God – the mercy that he figures as the 'root' of a single olive tree (Romans 11). Thus, despite sharp comments about Jews in a number of places, Paul does not think that God has given up on Israel. What has happened in Christ, the Messiah of Israel ('Christ' means Messiah), is for Paul the fulfilment of God's promises to Israel and to the nations. Although most of his fellow Jews did not yet believe in Christ, Paul was convinced that 'all Israel will be saved' (Romans 11.26).

Paul, in other words, works within the Jewish tradition, but with his own distinctive interpretation forged from his conviction that its defining moment had arrived. In fact, in his era there were many versions of Judaism, since Jews, under multiple cultural influences, interpreted their scriptural resources in a striking variety of ways. Contemporary to Paul were, for instance, the Jews of Qumran, authors of the Dead Sea Scrolls, according to whom Isaiah predicted their formation of a desert community, and their leader, the Teacher of Righteousness. At the same time, Philo, a Hellenized Jewish intellectual, was reading the Scriptures in Alexandria through a philosophical lens, finding in Moses the essential truths about the soul and its journey to the vision of God that (in his view) Plato had later rediscovered. Such diversity reflects the fact that in the preceding four centuries the peoples of the eastern end of the Mediterranean, including the Jews, had come under the influence of a mix of cultural traditions – Persian, Greek and Roman – reflecting a chequered political and social history. Thus, some educated Jews of Paul's time wrote Jewish apocalypses, depicting a universe full of competing spiritual forces and awaiting a cosmic upheaval; some wrote Stoic-inspired treatises on Jewish control of the passions; and some composed Greek plays about the life of Moses. At the less educated end of the spectrum, others wore Jewish-influenced amulets to ward off evil spirits.

Since there was no Jewish authority in Paul's day willing or able to impose a standard 'orthodoxy', there were many ways to be Jewish, and many interpretations of the Jewish tradition. Not all believed in a coming Messiah, but even those who did pictured the Messiah (or Messiahs) in various ways. Those who expected an end-time conversion of non-Jews imagined what that entailed in various forms. However, central to all forms of Judaism was respect for the Jerusalem Temple, which (until its destruction by the Romans in 70 CE) was famous throughout the world, visited by numerous Jewish pilgrims, and supported by an annual tax paid even by Jews who lived at a distance. Central also was allegiance to the Jewish Law, as revealed at Sinai, though there was plenty of room for dispute about what the Law meant and how it should be applied. In the Greek-speaking Diaspora, Hellenistic methods of interpretation, including allegory, found spiritual meanings hidden beneath the literal surface of the text; in other contexts, the literal application of legal rules to changed social circumstances caused considerable controversy. On the whole, however, it seems that there was a general Jewish consensus regarding those things that distinguished Jews and thus preserved their tradition down the generations. Core was the commitment to worship the one God alone and to allow no physical representation of this God – thus declining to participate in the standard religious practices that permeated Greek and Roman society. Associated with this commitment was a set of laws that labelled some foods unclean and made Jews generally wary of meals provided by non-Jews. Other distinctive Jewish practices were the observance of the Sabbath and the practice of male circumcision, the latter marking Jewish identity in a permanently physical form, and discouraging Jewish girls from marrying non-Jews.

Paul's interpretations of the Jewish Scripture were no more distinctive, in method or result, than those of his contemporary Jews. Although he spoke and wrote good Greek, his theology was less philosophically 'Hellenized' than that of many educated Diaspora Jews. What stands out as anomalous, however, are his attitudes to Jewish practice. In relation to 'idolatry' he was as uncompromising as his fellow Jews, although he thought that 'what you don't know can't hurt you' when it comes to buying meat that others might have sacrificed to a pagan deity (1 Corinthians 10). On food laws, however, he once declared that 'I know and am persuaded in the Lord Jesus that nothing is unclean in itself' (Romans 14.14). Although he protected those who kept kosher laws in honour of Christ, he labelled them 'weak' (in the sense of vulnerable), and aligned himself with the 'strong' who honoured Christ without such cultural limitations. The same goes for the observance of the Sabbath (discussed under the rubric of 'days' in Romans 14). Regarding male circumcision, he insisted that this must not be imposed on non-Jewish converts, and more than once declared it a matter of indifference (1 Corinthians 7.19; Galatians 5.6; 6.15), neither to be discarded nor to be sought. In each case, he considered it indifferent because it counted for less than something else.

That something else is what Paul calls 'new creation' (Galatians 6.15), the new reality that had emerged from the life, death and resurrection of Jesus Christ. Just after listing his considerable Jewish credentials, Paul speaks of 'the surpassing worth of knowing Messiah Jesus my Lord' (Philippians 3.3–8), in comparison with which his former gains are counted 'rubbish' and 'loss'. In other words, the Christ event, and Paul's experience of it through his 'calling in grace', has recalibrated his values, and has reoriented his interpretation of the Jewish tradition. We may trace the outlines of that revolution in two forms.

First, even Paul's understanding of God has been altered by his experience of Christ. It is not completely clear whether Paul expressly calls Jesus 'God' (Romans 9.5; scholars argue about the punctuation of the verse), but he strikingly reshapes the Jewish confession of 'one God' (the *Shema*: 'Hear, O Israel, the Lord our God is one Lord') by speaking of both 'one God' *and* 'one Lord', associating Jesus with God as if he were finding two figures (God and Lord) in the testimony to one God (1 Corinthians 8.6). Paul also declared Jesus to be 'the image of God' (after whom humanity was modelled, 2 Corinthians 4.4), and an early Paulinist soon developed this notion, representing Jesus as the one through whom, and for whom, all things were created (Colossians 1.15–20). Paul could not understand the life, death and resurrection of Jesus without seeing there the agency of God; but neither could he now understand God except in the light of what had happened in Christ.

Second, Paul understood the history of Israel and of the world in a different shape in the wake of the Christ-event.

As he reread Scripture he found pre-announcements of this event as early as the book of Genesis (Galatians 3.8), while discovering other echoes of his 'good news' in texts he would have read quite differently before. In the light of the resurrection of Jesus he interpreted his present as experiencing the 'down payment' of God's promises, the beginning of the final age that had been expected in the future. And he anticipated (soon) the return of Jesus to wrap up the history of the world, such that all the traditional Jewish images of the finale of history – judgement, resurrection and new creation – were reconfigured by reference to Christ.

What is more, throughout this history, past, present and future, Paul traced a pattern in God's dealings with humanity that was Christ-shaped in its emphasis on God's unconditioned grace. It was common in Judaism to celebrate the grace or mercy of God, but it was not so common to figure this mercy as given without regard to worth, since it would appear arbitrary or unfair for God to distribute the greatest benefits without some reference to the fittingness of their recipients. But Paul's own experience and the experience of his Gentile converts was that God paid no regard to human systems of social, moral or ethnic worth, and this alarmingly unexpected behaviour by God, demonstrated in Christ, shaped all Paul's convictions about history. He traced in the story of Abraham and in the history of Israel (Romans 4; 9—11) a pattern of unconditioned mercy that came to its climactic expression in Christ. In the present, he found this grace everywhere active in the calling of unworthy Gentiles into the people of God. And this gave Paul hope for the future, even for the presently 'disobedient' Jews who had not yet placed their trust in the Messiah Jesus. 'God has imprisoned all people in disobedience,' Paul concludes, 'in order that he may have mercy on all' (Romans 11.32). That is a reading of history that is simultaneously deeply scriptural and deeply indebted to Paul's experience of Christ.

Paul's reworking of the Jewish tradition, his allegiance to Christ, and his boundary-crossing experience of the Gentile mission resulted in a culturally ambiguous phenomenon, whose meaning was – and still is – heavily disputed. On the one hand, he saw his theology and his practices as deeply consistent with his Jewish heritage; on the other hand, the ways he reworked those traditions and relativized distinctive Jewish practices caused his Jewish contemporaries deep alarm. He identified with Israel and its future, but he found himself at odds with fellow Jews who did not believe in Christ and whom he considered (temporarily) 'cut off' from the olive tree to which they belonged (Romans 11). He could live like a Jew among Jews, but he could also disregard the Jewish Law out of allegiance to 'the Law of Christ', for the sake of his mission among non-Jews (1 Corinthians 9.19–23). Even as an apostle to non-Jews, he sometimes visited Jewish synagogues; but it is no surprise that he received there, five times, the heaviest punishment of a synagogue member, the 39 lashes (2 Corinthians 11.24). If such ambiguity caused criticism and confusion in Paul's own day, it has also evoked conflicting interpretations of Paul down through the centuries, not least when his views have been enlisted in deep disagreements over the relationship between Christianity and Judaism. We shall consider these readings in Chapter 9, below.

4

Paul's churches in the Roman world

Wherever Paul won converts who responded to his 'good news', he left behind little communities of believers, which he called *ekklēsiai* ('assemblies'). It is common to translate this word as 'churches', but we should be clear that the word denotes not a building but a gathering of people, usually meeting in homes, but in some cases, probably, in shops, public buildings or the open air.

Since Paul spent most of his time in major cities of the Roman Empire, his churches took root in multicultural environments with many temporary residents, which, then as now, were ideal contexts for people to undertake significant life changes. We do not know how many attended these gatherings, but where they met in homes they cannot have numbered more than thirty. It is probable that in large cities, like Rome, there were several 'house-churches' spread across the city or organized by family networks (see Romans 16). With one possible exception (Erastus in Corinth, Romans 16.23), none of their members was from the highest strata of society; the majority lived near subsistence level working, like Paul, for incomes that were never secure.

How should we place these 'assemblies' on the map of urban life in the Roman Empire? It helps to examine this map at three levels of increasing scale: the household, the city and the empire as a whole.

The household structure of Roman society was based on the family, but was different from modern families in the inclusion of three types of people: free people, slaves and freedmen (ex-slaves). Slavery was ubiquitous in cities, as in the countryside, and even households of modest means might own a slave or two to perform the most menial tasks. The majority of urban slaves were enslaved for life, and if a slave woman had children, whoever the father, these also belonged to the household as slaves. However, some slaves were manumitted (emancipated) as a reward for good service, and thereby became 'freedmen', and in some cases citizens, though they normally maintained personal, economic and social ties with their households. Authority structures were, in theory, highly stratified: the male head of the household had legal power (not always personal authority) over all other members, although at upper social levels married women retained control over their property, including their slaves. Marriage was the normal expectation, though it was common for men to marry later than women, creating an age gap between marriage partners that reinforced the gender inequality. Wives, who were generally not the only sexual partners of their husbands, were expected to start bearing children soon after marriage, often in their late teens; all too many died in the process. The majority of households lived at, or just above, subsistence level: ill health, accident, death or famine immediately tipped whole families into crisis, and, in the absence of safety nets, many lives were cut short by malnutrition or disease. In such perilous conditions, family members, across several generations, were the chief sources of support. Within households, an essential bond of unity was formed by common rituals devoted to household and ancestral gods, to whom prayers and sacrifices were offered for protection and prosperity.

The city was the matrix that held such households together, providing a common identity and a structure of political and economic leadership. Each city had its own proud history, but most of the Mediterranean cities where Paul worked had similar political and even architectural structures, overlaid by recent Roman additions. Politically and economically, the interests of citizens were preeminent, citizenship bringing legal privileges and at least notional political influence. But such was the importance of trade and the mobility it created that, at any one time, cities also contained numerous people who, like Paul, were only temporary residents. Both citizens and 'foreigners' might join one of the numerous voluntary associations or clubs that mushroomed in the urban environment – in most cases dining clubs in which local residents or people of the same occupation or ethnicity gathered for a monthly meal, paid for by subscription. Prominent here, as in any civic gathering, was worship of a patron deity, to whom an official would offer sacrifices and prayers for the flourishing of the association. On a wider scale, city officials, including priests, spent lavishly on grand temples, and the year was structured not by weeks but by festivals involving the whole citizen population, with processions, sacrifices and athletic or artistic competitions, in a carnival atmosphere designed to attract tourists and lift everyone's mood.

All the cities where Paul worked were already incorporated into the expanding Roman Empire, which had spread east through patronage of client kingdoms before imposing direct rule when it suited Rome's military and economic interests. Local civic authorities made a show of welcoming Roman presence, which added an upper layer of law, administration and taxation, and took most visual effect in the incorporation of Roman gods into civic religion and the addition of new temples. The emperor's image appeared everywhere, on coins and statues, on household goods and in civic processions, and worship was regularly offered to (or for) the emperor. Religion was inseparable from politics, because hierarchies of human power were understood to be supervised and legitimized by the overarching power of the gods.

Where did the Jewish people fit on this map? The Jewish homeland was, for most of Paul's life, under direct Roman rule through procurators answerable to the Roman governor of Syria. Experience had taught such procurators to interfere as little as possible with the Temple in Jerusalem, but Jewish festivals were major points of tension. Just as Jesus had been tried at a festival in Jerusalem by a Roman procurator (Pilate), Paul was arrested there during another festival by Roman troops sent from Caesarea to keep the peace. As we noted in Chapter 1, Paul spent many years in Caesarea awaiting and undergoing trials; if Acts is right, it was his appeal, as a Roman citizen, for trial before the emperor that led to his journey, under arrest, to Rome.

But this was a comparatively unusual phenomenon, as Paul was an unusually disruptive Jew. Most Jews in the Diaspora had learnt, through long experience, how to fit into local society without losing their distinct identity. Jewish life in the household was especially important. With a strong preference for endogamy (marrying within the ethnic group), Jewish marriages preserved ancestral traditions and maintained Jewish identity through the special rules around food and the observance of the Sabbath. Beyond the household, Jews formed ethnic associations (synagogues), equipped in some cases with their own buildings which advertised their presence and civic significance. Although some Jews melted into the religious environment of the city, most, it seems, preserved their identity by declining to worship civic deities, out of the unique Jewish aversion to the worship of any deity except the one God worshipped in the one Temple in Jerusalem. This self-exclusion from civic religion could cause controversy, but the Roman emperor and his local representatives normally permitted this exception and preserved Jewish rights, so long as Jews continued to make daily sacrifices in Jerusalem on behalf of the emperor. It was the cessation of these sacrifices that marked the start of the Jewish revolt in 66 CE, beginning the war that ended with the destruction of the Temple (70 CE) and a new, special tax on Jews throughout the empire.

How would Paul's little assemblies accommodate to this household, civic and imperial environment? The answer is, not very well.

With regard to the household, Paul, himself unmarried, advanced numerous arguments, theological and pragmatic, in favour of singleness (1 Corinthians 7). He did not, however, condemn marriage nor urge those married to seek divorce. This ambiguity led some later Paulinists (e.g. in Colossians and Ephesians) to Christianize marriage and household, along with their traditional structures, while others (e.g. the author of *The Acts of Paul and Thecla*) challenged Christian women to defy society by refusing marriage. Even where Paul's converts remained within the household structures, tensions could arise. It was easiest if the whole household became Christian believers at the same time, but if they did not, the solidarity of the household was threatened by competing forms of religious devotion. Since Christians adopted from their Jewish roots an intolerance towards pagan ('idolatrous') religion, friction with pagan spouses or masters was bound to arise. Where one partner was a believer and the other not, a marriage could come under strain (see 1 Corinthians 7.10–16; 1 Peter 3.1–6).

Moreover, even though the 'household codes' in Colossians and Ephesians urge deference to masters, husbands and fathers, they place all human authority under the superior rule of Christ. Slavery could create particular tensions in this regard. Neither Paul nor his imitators called for the emancipation of slaves, and Christian slave-owners were understandably reluctant to be deprived of slaves who were economic resources. But Paul did re-evaluate the slave as, like all others, given ultimate worth by the unconditioned call of God (1 Corinthians 7.17–24). He could even affirm that, following baptism, 'there is neither Jew nor Greek, there is neither slave nor free, there is no male and female, for you are all one in Christ Jesus' (Galatians 3.28). Precisely what that meant in practice was open to interpretation, and Paul's letter to Philemon shows the awkwardness that could arise. Onesimus, Philemon's unsatisfactory slave, had come to Paul for help, and through Paul had become a believer; that is, a 'brother'. When Paul sent him back to his owner, he presented Onesimus as a 'more than a slave, a beloved brother' (Philemon 16) and urged Philemon to receive Onesimus as he would receive Paul himself. This may not have resulted in the manumission of Onesimus, but the relationship between slave and master was complicated by their new relationship as 'brothers', a tension evidenced also elsewhere (1 Timothy 6.1–3). In other words, even where the Christian household was not altered structurally, supreme loyalty to Christ had the capacity to trump the values and expectations salient in the wider society (see Chapter 10).

But Christian difference was not always easy to demonstrate or to justify. Jewish households had food, Sabbath and circumcision practices to mark and maintain their difference, but the loyalty of Christian households to Jesus Christ was not buttressed by such regular and visible features. Worshipping Christ and abstaining from 'idolatry' constituted the most significant break with familial tradition, but, unlike Jews, Christian believers had no ancestral or ethnic rationale for this offensive religious difference. Already in Paul's earliest letter we can see the social and economic difficulties that accompanied 'turning to God from idols to serve the living and true God' (1 Thessalonians 1.9), and any such 'impious' and 'anti-social' behaviour would become particularly problematic at a civic level. In 1 Corinthians 8—10 Paul gives detailed instructions on the extent to which believers can, or cannot, eat food that others have sacrificed to 'idols'. But the text reveals that different believers in Corinth drew the line at different places, perhaps because some had too much to lose, socially and economically, in withdrawing from the occasions on which such food would be consumed. Paul wanted to keep social interaction possible, not least for the purposes of mission, but one can imagine the dilemmas of believers who were members of clubs where worship of a pagan deity was, strictly speaking, incompatible with their allegiance to Christ.

The members of Paul's churches were predominantly non-Jewish, and the more they were disowned or opposed by local Jews the more anomalous they looked on the social landscape of the Roman world. To abstain, without good reason, from normal religious activity was deeply offensive and even dangerous. It broke social solidarity and threatened the delicate relationship between the community and the gods, by which the safety of the community was maintained. This novel form of 'atheism' lacked any historical or cultural warrant, and could be interpreted as a direct affront to those in political authority. Paul himself was ambivalent about local civic authorities and about the Roman power that stood above them. He spoke disparagingly about 'the rulers of this age' who had crucified Jesus (1 Corinthians 2.6–8), and he hailed Jesus as the Lord of the cosmos whose power supersedes every power in the world: indeed, he looked forward to the time when 'at the name of Jesus every knee should bow' (Philippians 2.10). At the same time, when writing to Rome, he urges submission to the powers that be, not just on pragmatic grounds, but because they have been instituted by God (Romans 13.1–7). When he dismisses 'so-called gods' and 'so-called lords', he makes no special mention of the emperor or of the Roman pantheon of gods in which emperors were being incorporated (at least on death). But it is clear that, if it came to the crunch, Christians would have to be as unaccommodating to Roman religion as they were to any other form of 'idolatry'. It is likely that Paul's own execution in Rome was part of the Romans' discovery that Christians were social and religious misfits who would soon be made scapegoats for the great fire of Rome (64 CE). In any case, the challenge of the Christian movement to Roman religion, and its resistance to the visual propaganda and civic ritual that reinforced Roman rule, was ultimately to subvert, at a deep level, the whole edifice of Roman civilization.

5

Early images of Paul

Paul was a controversialist, capable of sharp, even crude polemics against his opponents. He had strong opinions, and was involved in numerous verbal fights, not least in face-to-face altercation with Peter (Galatians 2.11–14). He thereby made enemies, as well as friends, and there is evidence that many fellow believers, as well as non-believers, distrusted, disliked and opposed him. It was (and is) hard to be indifferent towards Paul: from the start, he has divided opinion more than anyone else in the early Christian movement.

A figure this controversial generates multiple images. Was he a fighter for the truth, against obstinate and malicious enemies, or a headstrong individualist who wilfully fractured the unity of the Church? Was he a visionary who saw most clearly the implications of the good news, or a dangerous extremist who led believers into blasphemous disregard of the Law of God? Paul himself was acutely aware of the rumours and criticisms that swirled in his wake. In Galatians he counters alternative versions of his own life history, in which he was portrayed as a wayward delegate of Jerusalem, insufficiently subordinate to Peter, James and John. In response, he presents his own account of events, including the independence of his calling and the agreement of these 'so-called pillars' to the terms of his mission (Galatians 2.1–10). He thus portrays himself as an embattled but triumphant warrior for 'freedom' and 'truth', complete with the scars that represent 'the marks of Jesus branded on my body' (Galatians 6.17).

In his letters to the Corinthians, Paul has to 'manage' his image on a different front. He had been overshadowed in Corinth by people with more impressive rhetorical skills (e.g. Apollos), and some Corinthian believers derided him as a weak figure, physically fragile, demeaned by his manual labour, and unable or unwilling to keep to his plans. 'His letters are weighty and strong,' they said, 'but his bodily presence is weak, and his speech contemptible' (2 Corinthians 10.10). In response, Paul merges skilful rhetoric with profound theology to offer an alternative image: he is, indeed, weak (too 'weak' to exploit the Corinthians, as others do), but that weakness is precisely what makes him a true messenger of Christ, whose power is made perfect in human weakness (2 Corinthians 12.9). By cataloguing his numerous vulnerabilities – the insults, hardships and persecutions he had endured – Paul takes on the appearance of a 'martyr', enduring anything for the sake of others and in defence of the truth. Ever conscious that he had once persecuted the Church, Paul finds in his story a paradigm of grace, while emphasizing that he, 'the least of the apostles' ('Paul' means 'little'), had worked harder than them all (1 Corinthians 15.10). Thus he constructs an image of himself as a hyper-dedicated, suffering apostle – an image that would render him heroic in the heated atmosphere of early Christianity, where persecution was taken to be the norm.

That heroized Paul is already evident in the Acts of the Apostles. This history of early Christianity was the companion volume to the Gospel attributed to Luke, dated by some scholars at the end of the first century (some of

Paul's journeys are narrated as if by a fellow traveller), and by others some decades into the second. In any case, the figure of Paul dominates this narrative to an extraordinary degree. His conversion is recounted no fewer than three times, profiling his role as *the* agent who brought the good news to the non-Jewish world. Practically all of the second half of this narrative is devoted to Paul's journeys, sermons, escapades and trials. Here Paul is profiled as a preacher, a miracle-worker and a martyr. Lengthy Scripture-laced sermons are attributed to Paul, typically resulting in his expulsion from a synagogue; elsewhere, a set-piece speech to the intellectuals of Athens is larded with philosophical allusions (Acts 17). As a fearless but versatile preacher, Paul becomes a paradigm of Christian communication in a hostile or sceptical world. But the narrative is also lightened, and enlivened, by vivid episodes of miraculous power: Paul heals the sick, escapes imprisonment, and is saved, with the crew, from a dramatic shipwreck. The narrative is clearly heading towards Paul's death, although it ends before that climax: his farewell speech in Ephesus (Acts 20) indicates that his journey to Rome will be his last. The lengthy but inconclusive trials correct Paul's reputation as a renegade Jew or a subversive Roman, but they point forwards towards a Roman miscarriage of justice that Luke may have preferred not to recount. The gap at the end of this story would be filled by others, but Luke had already done enough to cement the image of Paul as a model martyr (successor to Jesus and Stephen), who went to his death for the sake of the truth.

One aspect of Paul's image that Luke does *not* portray is Paul the writer of letters. Others, as we have seen (Chapter 2), developed that profile by writing new letters in his name. By this means it was possible to adopt his literary persona in order to develop the message of his letters (2 Thessalonians, adapting 1 Thessalonians), or to summarize and generalize his teaching in a form no longer tied to local crises (Ephesians). And when Paul's churches developed multiple versions of Christian theology and practice, it was necessary to personify Paul as a community organizer, ensuring that authorized teachers would clarify and preserve the truth (1 Timothy and Titus). These pseudonymous letters cement or adapt the earlier images of Paul and create new profiles. In Ephesians, Paul's central role in the Gentile mission is now presented on a cosmic scale, where the spread of the Church (singular) to the whole human race is the earthly counterpart to the Christ who fills and completes the universe. Here also Paul's dangerous preference for celibacy is muted by a household code that makes marriage a sign of the relation between Christ and the Church (Ephesians 5—6). The letter 2 Timothy paints an intimate portrait of Paul awaiting death, anxious for the Church and largely abandoned by his friends, but facing his end with confidence that God will grant him his reward (2 Timothy 4.6–18). This lonely but heroic figure underlines the importance of 'orthodox' truth, at a time when there were no generally agreed criteria to determine the Christian faith and its practical implications.

In fact, Paul himself could be made to speak for many versions of truth. In *The Acts of Paul and Thecla* he is a preacher of sexual asceticism and an opponent of marriage – an image with echoes of 1 Corinthians 7 but diametrically opposed to the Paul of Ephesians or 1 Timothy. *The Acts of Paul and Thecla* was probably composed in the middle of the second century, but quickly became popular, as much for its image of Thecla (the real heroine of the interlaced narratives) as for its image of Paul. In an ironic inversion of a love-romance, Thecla, a wealthy girl from Antioch (in Pisidia), is entranced by Paul who blesses those who renounce the flesh and commit themselves to celibacy. Thecla accordingly breaks off her engagement, much to the horror of her fiancé and her mother. In the tales that follow, Thecla is condemned to public execution on more than one occasion, and escapes death only by divine intervention. One gains here a vivid sense of how isolated and vulnerable an unmarried Christian girl might be.

This image of a socially radical Paul is fittingly completed in *The Martyrdom of Paul*, a text early associated with *The Acts of Paul and Thecla*. Here the gap at the end of the Acts of the Apostles is filled with a vivid description of Paul's execution, the symbol of a head-on collision between the Roman emperor and the 'soldiers' of Christ. Paul thus represents a refusal to compromise, socially or politically, with the mores of the Roman world: the option for celibacy is the wedge that prises open the radical difference in orientation between those who support the Roman status quo and those who march to a different, counter-cultural tune. The popularity of these tales supported a widespread Christian conviction that the control, and even the eradication, of sexual desire was a fundamental marker of Christian difference, a symbol of their stance against 'the world'.

A related kind of radical Paul was the hero of another second-century version of Christianity, shaped by Marcion, an intellectual in the church at Rome. Marcion was convinced that Christianity had become compromised since its first generation; there was only one authoritative apostle, and that was Paul. Putting ten letters of Paul into a collection (he may not have known of the Pastorals), and joining them to a single Gospel (a 'restored' Gospel of Luke), Marcion presented Paul as the figure who had uniquely, by revelation, understood the truth about Christ and the freedom he had brought. Jesus Christ was the Son of the greater and previously unknown God, distinct from the God who had created the flawed physical world; the latter was the God worshipped by Jews, and known through the Jewish Scriptures. Putting Galatians at the head of his Pauline collection, Marcion highlighted the salvation of believers 'from the present evil age' (Galatians 1.4), since Christ had brought a 'new creation' in which they were 'crucified to the world' (Galatians 6.14–15). Paul, he thought, made reference to the inferior, Creator God, who was liable to judge and even damage humanity, when he spoke of 'the god of this age who has blinded the minds of the unbelievers' (2 Corinthians 4.4). At the centre of Marcion's theology stood Paul's references to God's love, reinforced by Luke's image of a graciously inclusive Jesus, a perfect love that could never condemn or punish humanity. Marcion relished Paul's self-image as a lonely fighter for truth, and took Paul's enemies to represent those who, both in Paul's day and since, had attempted to dilute the pure gospel with inferior Jewish traditions. Paul the controversialist had become, for Marcion, the key resource by which to rescue the Church from its compromising reverence for the poor theology of the Jewish Scriptures.

Marcion's image of Paul was based on careful reading of Paul's letters, at least those parts that had not (in his view) been 'corrupted' by later additions (such as positive citations of the Old Testament). Other schools of thought in second-century Christianity were also enamoured of Paul, whose theology (combined with the Gospel of John) they took to validate a 'spiritualized' understanding of salvation, as the enlightenment and liberation of the true self from its bodily imprisonment in a faulty, material universe. Were not the believers blessed with every *spiritual* blessing, and chosen *before* the foundation of the (material) world (Ephesians 1.3–4)? Were they not already saved through association with the risen Christ, by a grace that granted the fullness of knowledge (Ephesians 2.5–6; 3.14–19)? And was not resurrection described by Paul as 'spiritual' (1 Corinthians 15.44)? Such are the emphases in a number of texts associated with a Christian intellectual named Valentinus, traditionally labelled a 'gnostic' theologian.

The opponents of Marcion and of the 'gnostics' were clearly embarrassed by such well-informed interpretation of the letters of Paul. They could not challenge the authority of Paul, but were obliged to provide an alternative image of Paul and different readings of his letters. Thus Irenaeus (*c.*130–200) and Tertullian (*c.*160–225) responded to Marcion and to advocates of a 'falsely called knowledge' with an image of a more consensual Paul – a trustworthy apostle, but only one among others, including the Jerusalem authorities. Marcion's pure 'Paulinism' was to them a threatening phenomenon, since its abstraction of his theology from its larger scriptural matrix produced a dangerously one-sided version of Christian theology. In this maelstrom of second-century debate, the image of Paul was a central matter of dispute. In his letters, Paul's profile is angular and sharp. That profile could be softened and romanticized in a number of ways, but it could also be sharpened still further, or re-angled, to address new controversies. Almost everybody wanted a piece of Paul. The question was which

Paul they would present, or fashion, for their current purposes. If Paul was too important to ignore, he was also too ambiguous a figure easily to be contained in a single image or a singular interpretation. The stage is set for the long, rippling effect of multiple Pauls through Christian history and theology.

Part 2

THE LEGACY

6

Paul as Scripture

A text written in the name of Peter in the early second century expresses an intriguing perception of the letters of Paul:

> So also our beloved brother Paul wrote to you according to the wisdom given to him, speaking of this [proper preparation for the day of the Lord] as he does in all his letters. There are some things in them hard to understand, which the ignorant and unstable twist to their own destruction, as they do the other scriptures.   (2 Peter 3.15–16)

Several features of this statement typify the reception of Paul's letters from the second century onwards: they are difficult to construe; they are authoritative, with the status of 'Scripture'; their interpretation is controversial; and so high are the stakes in such interpretation that salvation itself is at risk.

What made Paul's letters so 'hard to understand'? Sometimes there are ambiguities embedded in his language. When he said that 'the *telos* of the law is Christ' (Romans 10.4), did he mean the *end* of the law, or its *fulfilment*? The Greek could be construed either way. (Centuries later, the Lutheran tradition leaned one way, the Calvinist tradition the other.) Statements in Paul's letters on the resurrection could, from a later perspective, fit either of two opposing viewpoints. Does 'resurrection' life after death involve a reconstituted body? Paul had spoken mysteriously of a 'spiritual body', while stating that 'flesh and blood cannot inherit the kingdom of God' (1 Corinthians 15.44, 50). For many interpreters in the second century, this indicated that the spirit would be relieved of the present physical body (*spiritual* body meaning non-physical); for others, a spiritual *body* indicated that the present body would be supernaturally restored and renewed, while the exclusion of 'flesh and blood' meant only the eradication of sinful bodily desires. Both sides insisted that Paul supported their theologies of the body, and each considered the other both 'ignorant' and 'unstable'. The fact that Paul himself was so polemical in style encouraged his readers to follow suit.

What is more, because Paul's letters are not systematic treatises (see Chapter 2), he may use the same term (e.g. 'the law') in different senses in different contexts, such that later interpreters could select or emphasize one use over another. Even in his own day, Paul had to challenge what he considered misinterpretations of what he had written (1 Corinthians 5.9), and once he was no longer around to 'correct' his readers, alternative readings could multiply. Sometimes Paul's letters contain hidden presuppositions that require interpreters to fill in the gaps: when he suggests that women should have their heads covered 'because of the angels' (1 Corinthians 11.10), interpreters are left guessing how angels are involved. And then there is Paul's love of paradox. What did he mean when he said, 'I have been crucified with Christ; it is no longer I who live but Christ who lives in me'? And how can he then continue, 'And the life I now live in the flesh . . .' (Galatians 2.19–20)? In what sense was he 'crucified' with Christ? In what sense is it no longer 'I' but Christ who lives? And who is the 'I' that now 'lives in the flesh'? From this set of puzzles there arise deep questions about Christian existence and the identity of the self, questions that require the use of some theological or philosophical framework. But which is the best to apply?

If Paul was 'hard to understand', he was also authoritative, and the greater the authority the more awkward the difficulty in the task of understanding. Paul's letters are compared in our 2 Peter text with 'the other scriptures', and it appears that by this time his letters had gained a status equal to what Jews and Christians called 'the Scriptures', and what Christians have since named 'The Old Testament'. When the early Christians supplemented these 'Scriptures' with their own texts, selecting, copying and circulating a number of gospels and letters, Paul's letters constituted a large section of their top choices (what we now call 'The New Testament'). Scriptural status entailed special reading practices and raised high expectations. It invited close study and prolonged reflection, especially when the well-educated were charged with teasing out the meaning of these texts for the benefit of all. Placing Paul's letters in this category also led interpreters to expect some level of internal coherence – not only between the Pauline letters but also between them and the other parts of Scripture. And where Paul was taken to sing in harmony, even if not in unison, with other voices in Scripture, some possible meanings might be closed off, but other, new meanings, could be heard. Whether Paul's voice in this choir is subordinate to that of the Gospels (as is common in the Catholic tradition), or whether he stands out as the soloist with whom others are expected to harmonize (as is typical in the Protestant tradition), is a significant variable underlying different receptions of Paul down to this day.

Scriptural status also implied that Paul was expected to speak to the *present* of the interpreter. Paul-as-Scripture was taken to be a medium for the Spirit or the Word of God, and thus not bound to Paul's own lifetime, however much historical knowledge might contribute to the interpretation of his letters. The fullest engagement with Paul has arisen in those spheres where Paul's voice in the canon is most rich and weighty. The pastoral dimensions of his letters – his moral and practical instructions on such matters as sexual morality, church community and life in the Spirit – are of a range and depth to provide endless resources for preachers and church-builders throughout the centuries. But Paul's biggest imprint has been in the scope with which he portrays the narrative of salvation, and the depth with which he interprets its meaning at both personal and social levels. In this domain, he was the original and perhaps the most fertile Christian theologian of all time, and his legacy has been immense.

Paul's vision spans from before the very beginning of time to its end in eternity. His human history starts with Adam (whom he understood quite literally as the first human being) and climaxes in the return ('the coming') of Christ. He probably thought that he was living in the last generation of this history, but later interpreters could extend this timeline up to and beyond their own day, while keeping most other features of his theology intact. Paul's long arc of salvation included the history of Israel as recounted in the Scriptures. Certain episodes in this history took on, for Paul, paradigmatic significance, but his ability to discover lessons throughout these Scriptures, and to apply them even to his Gentile converts, gave crucial hermeneutical clues to later readers of the Bible. And since the scope of salvation, for Paul, extended as wide as the cosmos, founded in God's mysterious plan (Ephesians 1), and led towards its 'liberation' (Romans 8), Paul has provided theologians with tools for interpreting time and space on the widest possible scale.

Matching this breadth of vision is the depth of Paul's analysis of the human condition. No other New Testament texts have such extensive, and such intriguing, statements about human beings and their problematic condition. Central here is Paul's language of 'sin', which he sometimes uses to speak of acts of transgression ('sins' in the plural) and sometimes with reference to a power that holds humanity in its grip ('Sin' in the singular). In this regard, the triple depiction of sin in Paul's letter to the Romans (in chapters 1—3, 5 and 7) has been widely influential. Here the human condition is painted on an expressly universal canvas: 'all, both Jews and Greeks [= non-Jews], are under Sin' (Romans 3.9), for 'all have sinned and lack the glory of God' (Romans 3.23). The nexus of Sin, judgement and death is then traced across human history, from Adam onwards (Romans 5.12–21), and, in a particularly memorable passage, an 'I' is portrayed as perpetually frustrated in its attempts to do good by Sin's operations through 'the law' (Romans 7.7–25). In subsequent Christian tradition, sin has been interpreted in multiple ways – as disordered desire, as the work of the Devil, as selfish pride or simply as our mysterious propensity to mess things up – but at the root of most of these theories lies the varied discourse of Romans.

Matching this complex analysis of the human condition, Paul has supplied many of the central Christian metaphors for salvation. Justification (from the language of law), redemption and liberation (from the field of slavery), expiation (from rituals of sacrifice), blessing, life, adoption, participation 'in Christ' – all these have provided a large store of concepts by which the meaning of salvation can be explored. By and large, the Western Christian tradition has gravitated towards Paul's cultic and legal metaphors, as refracted through Augustine. In the Eastern tradition, under the influence of John Chrysostom and the Cappadocian Fathers (Basil the Great, Gregory of Nyssa and Gregory of Nazianzus, from the fourth century), metaphors of 'transformation' and 'renewal' have been dominant, with the believer drawn upwards towards participation in God through the Spirit. Paul's language is sufficiently malleable to fit several philosophical perspectives, and his understanding of salvation, and thus of human fulfilment, has been given a variety of philosophical accents: Stoic, (neo-) Platonist or Aristotelian, and, in modern times, Hegelian or existentialist.

Interpretation is not just repetition. However much interpreters have wanted to remain 'faithful' to Paul, none has simply repeated what he has said. Even translating his words into another language is an act of interpretation, but so also is the selection of texts, and the decision about which texts to prioritize over others. The truth is, no one reads 'from nowhere': inevitably and properly, all interpreters of a text (*any* text) bring their own interests, concerns, contexts and personalities *to* the text, even as they strive to let the text challenge their presuppositions. In this sense, an interpretation of a text bears some resemblance to the performance of a play: there will be something fresh, and newly meaningful, in a good contemporary performance, however ancient the script and however 'accurately' performed. This 'contemporizing' takes place even in those interpretations of Paul's letters that claim to be purely historical 'reconstructions', but it is overtly and properly present wherever these texts function as Scripture. Christian readers of Paul, as of the rest of the Bible, have generally felt themselves responsible for keeping this text 'alive' in their own generation, however conscious they may be that it originated in a long-distant past.

Thus, Paul's legacy continues to pay out dividends, year on year, without depletion of its initial capital: there is a sense of surplus, but also of constant dependence on the original deposit. Theological interpreters of Paul have sometimes been guilty of overriding the text – limiting its meaning or manipulating it as a flimsy cover for their own theological agendas. But often one gets the opposite sense, that they discover in the text an extraordinary range of possible meanings, a seemingly endless 'semantic potential'. Thus, the history of interpretation of these letters is not best understood as a centuries-long search for the one, original meaning, for which historical experts search as the ultimate 'holy grail'. Rather, interpreters in each generation and in every new context have entered into deep conversations with these texts, exploring diverse possibilities of meanings which will never be singular, final or fixed. Those conversations will not cease so long as Paul is recognized as a potent voice within the cultural traditions of the (Western) world, or, if that ceases, so long as the Christian Scriptures continue to be read by a receptive and reflective Church.

7

Augustine and the Western Church

Christian history underwent a fundamental change when the Roman Emperor Constantine converted to Christianity (312 CE). Soon the Roman state began to give financial and political support to churches, and Roman society and culture were slowly but surely 'Christianized'. As churches grew and attracted a higher percentage of the educated elite, the Christian Scriptures gained the status of a core cultural text, and Paul's letters were heard throughout the Roman world and across all social levels in church services and sermons. Paul was a particular favourite of John Chrysostom (347–407), one of the finest orators of his day; his powerful sermons on Paul's letters, delivered in Antioch and Constantinople, are still hugely influential in Orthodox churches. In the Latin-speaking West, a number of fourth-century intellectuals wrote commentaries on Paul, but one figure towers above them all, both in the depth of his engagement with Paul and in his influence on subsequent Western theology: Augustine of Hippo (354–430).

Augustine was one of the most brilliant men of his generation, with a mind highly trained in both rhetoric and philosophy. Although his mother, Monica, was a Christian, he was initially a member of the Manichaean movement – a hybrid of Christian and Zoroastrian traditions, which used the antithetical structures of Paul's thought to posit two opposing cosmic powers that determined the fate of human beings. This offered a clear explanation for the origin of evil – an issue with which Augustine grappled throughout his life. His conversion to Christianity, charted in his *Confessions*, required him to reframe his theological questions, and to seek new answers, and in that quest the reading and rereading of Paul's letters became the single most shaping factor in Augustine's theology. Although some of the extremes to which he was led were highly controversial both in his lifetime and thereafter, he shaped the Western reading of Paul to such an extent that all medieval and Reformation interpretations of Paul constitute developments of the Augustinian tradition, even when they differ from him in significant ways.

Augustine took Paul (and especially his letter to the Romans) as depicting the universal story of humanity, stretching from the original creation (Romans 1) to the final and eternal restoration of all things (Romans 8). The universal plight in which we live is not imposed by external forces but is the effect of human sin – the original sin of Adam that has affected all humanity ever since (Romans 5). Following Paul's language of law, Augustine interpreted this sin primarily as disobedience, which is deservedly punished by God. But his distinctive contribution was to trace the origin of this disobedience to the pride and wilful self-dependence that lurk in the inner recesses of the human heart. The essence of sin, for Augustine, is to wish to be like God (Genesis 3.5); that is, to give credit to oneself and not to God. This framework shaped the way Augustine read the Pauline antithesis between 'faith in Christ' and 'works of the law' (Galatians 2.16; Romans 3.19–31; 9.30—10.4). Augustine's contemporary, Jerome (*c.*342–420), followed the hitherto common opinion that 'works of the law' meant

Jewish cultural practices (e.g. Sabbaths, circumcision and food laws), which were rendered obsolete by Christ. Augustine considered that interpretation inadequate: Paul had no objection to Jewish believers continuing such practices, and what was really at stake was not the practices themselves but the attitude of pride that accompanied them. Augustine emphasized the language of 'boasting' that Paul uses in this context (e.g. in Romans chapters 2—4), while noting that such boasting could concern 'works' in general and not just the specific-sounding 'works of the law' (e.g. Romans 3.27; 4.1–5; 11.6; Ephesians 2.8–9). In other words, the error Paul attacked was not doing the wrong things (outdated Jewish practices), but doing even the right things with pride, attributing virtue to oneself. God's grace, Augustine insists, is given without regard to merit, and it is the deepest form of sin to claim credit for one's own achievements.

If we are created by a good God, and therefore created good, why would we fall into such a perverse error? Here Augustine utilized Paul's terminology to analyse the depths of the human will, our motivating desires. Our proper, created, desire is to seek God, in humble dependence on our Creator as the source of every good. Human sin is the perversion of those desires, not only in seeking the material above the spiritual, but in turning in upon ourselves, perverting love for God (the root of proper love for others) into love for ourselves and the gratification of our selfish desires. Augustine was fascinated by Romans 7, and the depiction there of the 'I' who wants to do good, but continually does the opposite, subject to a seemingly inbuilt tendency to reject what is good and pursue what is wrong. He was impressed by the fact that Paul there depicts the law as somehow exacerbating this problem (Romans 7.7–13) and, in a memorable illustration, remembered his own boyhood delight in stealing pears from a tree – an act that was all the more pleasurable for being expressly forbidden. Paul singles out the command, 'you shall not desire' (Romans 7.7), one of the ten commandments, and an echo of 'the fall' (Genesis 3.6). Augustine himself had battled long and unsuccessfully with sexual desire, and he was impressed by the fact that male sexual arousal could be involuntary. If this disruptive desire was that deeply rooted in the human psyche, it was not just the result of the conscious will. Since it was the tradition in the North African church to baptize newborn babies, church practice also suggested that the guilt and power of sin were somehow endemic from birth. Following the Latin translation of Romans 5.12 ('sin came into the world through one man . . . in whom all sinned'), Augustine thought that guilt for sin was inherited from Adam's original transgression, and was passed down the generations through procreation. After all, none of us would have been born without the lust that brought our parents into sexual union.

The essence of the gospel could be summed up, for Augustine, in one word: grace (Latin: *gratia*). He took this to be the chief topic of Paul's letter to the Romans, and the ways he explored and developed this theme, sometimes to extremes, have shaped both Catholic and Protestant theology to this day. Grace is the chief antidote to pride since, as Paul says (in a text Augustine repeatedly cites), 'What do you have that you did not receive?' (1 Corinthians 4.7). Grace is not just a gift or favour, but a power that enters deeply into human agency, even into the human will. How are our perverse wills able at all to turn from ourselves to God? In one of Augustine's favourite texts (he cites it more than 200 times, and echoes it countless times more), Paul had written that 'the love of God has been poured into our hearts through the Holy Spirit that has been given to us' (Romans 5.5). Augustine usually took 'the love of God' here to refer to our love for God: in other words, we cannot love God (that is, be restored to our proper relation to God) unless this love is infused into our hearts by God himself, through the agency of his Spirit. All of our virtue is, at core, effected by the gracious agency of God.

Augustine was careful to preserve the language of human 'free will', but he found reason in Paul to put emphasis on the agency of God who works not only in our actions but also in our wills: 'God is at work in you both to will and to work for a good will' (as the Latin translates Philippians 2.13). The question of the relationship between grace and free will was controversial, however, and became famously sharp in Augustine's bitter disputes with Pelagius, a well-educated British monk. Pelagius took exception to Augustine's language, and insisted that the grace of God, which creates our capacity to do good, and gives us every incentive to do it, does not encroach on our human responsibility for doing good or evil. In this heated and polarizing debate, Augustine turned 'Pelagian' into an adjective that has ever after been associated with an inadequate view of grace. But the issues were difficult, and the more Augustine reflected on the efficacy of divine grace, the more he developed Paul's language of predestination. Paul's letters refer to election and predestination (e.g. Romans 8.28), even 'before the foundation of the world' (Ephesians 1.4), and in a notorious passage that puzzled all interpreters of Paul there are suggestions that some are destined for salvation and others for 'destruction' (Romans 9.6–26). For Augustine, such notions should be taken with full seriousness. All humans are fittingly destined for destruction on account of God's just punishment of sin; but by the mysterious operation of grace, and through no virtue of their own, some are chosen for eternal life. Paul himself considered God's mercy a mystery (Romans 11.33–36), and Augustine was inclined to leave it at that.

Augustine's radical interpretations of grace were a possible but not a necessary reading of Paul, and they created considerable tensions with other parts of Scripture. Towards the end of his life, even some of his admirers thought he had gone too far, and since his day theologians have often pulled back from some of his most extreme conclusions. But few have challenged his Paul-derived claim that grace is central to Christian doctrine and to the Christian life. Exactly how grace relates to 'nature', to 'free will' and to 'merit' would be matters of debate for centuries to come, but the Pauline notion that God's undeserved grace is somehow constitutive of the very being of a believer would reverberate through history in the precise and powerful rhetoric of Augustine. Augustine's genius was to connect this motif to the personal experience of the ordinary believer. Just as Paul had said, 'by the grace of God I am what I am' (1 Corinthians 15.10), Augustine could relate grace to the struggles of believers, who daily, in the Lord's Prayer, ask for forgiveness and divine aid. Augustine's own deep spirituality, and his involvement, as bishop, with complex pastoral problems meant that his doctrine could not be dismissed as armchair theology. His powerful personality and brilliant polemics may, like a megaphone, have altered the tenor of Paul's voice, but they have made Paul audible for centuries of further Christian reflection.

Augustine's influence ensured that Paul's letters played a major role in Western medieval theology. Anselm of Canterbury (*c.*1033–1109) developed Paul's depiction of the death of Christ as sacrifice (Romans 3) to explain how this death satisfied God's judgement and absorbed God's wrath in the place of sinful humanity. Paul's mystical experiences (2 Corinthians 12.1–4), combined with his talk of 'sharing in his [Christ's] sufferings, becoming like him in his death' (Philippians 3.10), influenced many forms of Christian mysticism, while his preference for celibacy (1 Corinthians 7) inspired Christian asceticism, not least that practised by monks. But, following Augustine, Paul was especially honoured as a theologian, with a reputation for intellectual depth and systematic coherence. The 'scholastic' theologians, who have an unjustified reputation for obsession with minutiae, were concerned to place all truth – scientific, philosophical and historical – within the frame of Christian faith. Since Paul's letters cover the gamut of nature, history, epistemology, salvation and eschatology, his voice was important in this endeavour, but the pressure to make Christian doctrine comprehensive and systematic was bound to squeeze Paul into some unfamiliar shapes. The *Sentences* of Peter Lombard (*c.*1100–60) and the *Summa Theologica* of Thomas Aquinas (*c.*1225–74) are two of the most influential medieval efforts to create from Christianity a total intellectual system. Texts and motifs from Paul are woven through these works, but they are necessarily interlaced with other scriptural threads and with Christian interpretations of philosophy. For some subsequent theologians, this was the only proper way to acknowledge Paul's scriptural authority; for others, this procedure blunted the radical sharpness of his thought. Like many scholastics, both Lombard and

Aquinas also wrote commentaries on the letters of Paul, in which they endeavour, but sometimes struggle, to relate the specificity of these letters to their own larger scriptural and theological frameworks. There is always the danger that, in being pressed to speak on matters of Christian doctrine that do not match his concerns, Paul's voice gets misconstrued. Precisely because of his importance to the Christian theological tradition, his letters may be required to bear a weight they cannot sustain.

Nowadays some regard the very attempt to make Paul a systematic theologian wholly misconceived: his situational first-century letters, with their 'jumpy' logic and exaggerated rhetoric, constitute a genre of theology that cannot be translated into the cool rationality of a doctrinal system. From this perspective, Augustine's interpretation of Paul's theology may look like an anachronistic imposition on the original Paul, imputing to him questions about the self, the will and the conscience that were far from his mind. But, as we have seen, interpretation of such seminal texts cannot be confined to rediscovery of their 'original meaning'. However much one agrees or disagrees with the legacy of Augustine, it is hard to deny that his conversation with Paul was rich, profound, and of far-reaching significance for Western theology and culture.

8

Paul in the Protestant tradition

The central role accorded to Paul by the sixteenth-century reformers has ensured that Protestantism is to a large extent 'Pauline' in theology, liturgy and spirituality. Although Paul's statements on baptism and the Lord's Supper, on union with Christ and resurrection, are influential right across the Christian Church, the attempt to frame the whole biblical canon, and to shape the whole of Christian theology, in Pauline terms is a distinctively Protestant endeavour.

Martin Luther (1483–1546) elevated the authority of Scripture (newly accessible in its original Hebrew and Greek) above every other Christian authority, traditional or institutional, but it was the letters of Paul that provided the key with which to interpret both the Old Testament and the New. Even the Gospels were subordinated to Paul inasmuch as the life and teaching of Jesus were to be understood, first and foremost, under the Pauline rubric of 'gift'. Luther was drawn to Paul for many reasons. Paul's sharp polemics suited his cast of mind, since Luther also thought that he lived in an 'apocalyptic' era when the truth of the gospel was engaged in a final battle with a deeply deceptive alternative. Paul's stark antithesis between the cross of Jesus and human 'wisdom' or 'strength' (1 Corinthians 1.18–31; Galatians 6.14–15) fuelled Luther's rejection of the Aristotelian philosophy that had shaped medieval theology, fostering a clear polarity between divine gift and human achievement. Luther absorbed deeply Paul's emphasis on the incongruity between divine grace and human worth, developing this Augustinian theme into a full-frontal attack on the ideology of merit that was the foundation of religious practice in the medieval church. Paying for indulgences, commissioning Masses for the sake of the dead, honouring chastity and poverty as superior Christian callings, even the practice of the Mass as sacrifice to God – all these represented for Luther the performance of 'works' for the sake of gaining the favour of God either in this life or the next. But Paul, Luther insisted, pitted faith *against* 'works' (or 'works of the law') when it came to justification or salvation: faith grasps the gift of Christ, already fully and freely given without regard to merit, while 'works' represent the erroneous opinion, and sinful confidence, that human deeds are a means by which to gain salvation. In fact, Paul's negative statements about 'the law' encouraged Luther to develop a broad antithesis between 'law' and 'gospel': law represents God's just demand, which exposes our deep sinfulness but cannot rescue us from this plight; gospel is the good news that God has already given us in Christ all things necessary for salvation.

Luther realized that he was applying Paul's language to a new context, but he took Paul's situation to be providentially close to his own. Paul's letter to the Galatians was his favourite, 'my Katharina von Bora' (his wife). There Paul resisted the pressure to make non-Jews adopt the Mosaic Law (see above, Chapter 2) by the antithesis between 'faith in Christ' and 'works of the law' that Luther took to be exactly what was at stake in his day. There also Paul battled heroically against the error of Peter, just as Luther challenged the authority of Peter's successor, the Pope. Paul's language of 'justification' was given a radical new reading: Paul is not speaking about God *making us righteous*, by moral transformation, but of God *regarding us as righteous* inasmuch as we are united to Christ by faith. In ourselves we remain flawed and sinful beings; but in Christ we are justified ('at the same time justified and a sinner'). Such a paradox reflects Luther's attraction to Paul's paradoxical expressions ('it is no longer I who live, but Christ who lives in me', Galatians 2.20), which suggested that paradox was the only way in which we can understand God and the anomalous condition of believers. Paul's highly personal language was also important to Luther, because faith, as repeated return to dependence on God's undeserved grace, has to be exercised by each individual, even if it is strengthened by the communal activities of worship, preaching and the Lord's Supper. The recognition by each believer, of whatever status or condition, that Christ died 'for me' (Galatians 2.20) has formed the emotional core of Protestant spirituality ever since.

Luther took Paul's theology of grace to liberate Christians from their anxious concern to gain God's favour so that they could give themselves freely and unselfishly to others. In this cascade of grace, willing service for the neighbour could be given without need or expectation of return, an emphasis that has contributed to Western notions of the 'pure gift'. And since there were no callings in life that made one nearer to God, whether through sexual abstinence or voluntary poverty, Luther made all social and economic vocations of equal value as an arena for Christian service. Against the long tradition by which Paul's advice on celibacy (1 Corinthians 7) had been taken to rank chastity above marriage, Luther renounced his monastic vows, married a nun, had numerous children, and celebrated the earthiness of marriage and family life. By raising the status of the ordinary duties of family, work and civic obligations (in line with the household codes of Colossians and Ephesians), Luther aimed to 'sacralize' the whole of life, without hierarchies of spiritual importance. This shift was arguably one impetus towards modern notions of equality and democracy, although some now regard it, in hindsight, as a step that led, unintentionally, towards the secularization of the West.

John Calvin (1509–64) was an equally Paul-centred interpreter of Scripture; he once described Paul's letter to the Romans as 'an open door to all the most profound treasures of Scripture'. Equipped by the methods and skills of classical scholarship, Calvin wrote commentaries on all of Paul's letters (and subsequently, on most of the Bible), but also synthesized the theologies of the Bible, viewed through a Pauline lens, in his *Institutes of the Christian Religion*. Paul's contrast between the 'old and 'new' covenants (2 Corinthians 3) was used by Calvin to provide an overarching historical schema, in which the history of Israel looked forward to the final revelation of grace in Christ. Calvin's urge to provide a comprehensive theology extended Pauline motifs across the whole map of theology, with immense influence on Christian culture in the Reformed (Calvinist) tradition ever since.

Calvin adopted much of Luther's revolutionary thinking on grace and justification, but added distinctive accents. To the grace of justification he added the subsequent grace of 'sanctification' (another Pauline term), and this emphasis on holiness, as a progressive discipline of the Christian life, gave meaning to a believer's biography as a journey of spiritual development. Drawing on Romans 9 and on the later texts of Augustine, Calvin developed a strong doctrine of election which was designed to give confidence to believers, but also encouraged them to look, sometimes anxiously, for 'signs' of their election. Whether or to what extent these Calvinist emphases lie behind the 'Protestant work ethic' and the rise of capitalism (as in Max Weber's famous thesis) is still disputed. But there can be little doubt that Puritan introspection, the disciplines of daily piety and the concern to chart spiritual progress – key features of much British, and then American, Protestant spirituality – are direct descendants of Calvin's reading of Paul.

The political tensions that accompanied the Reformation forced the Reformers to question anew how the Church should relate to the state, and here again Paul's legacy was significant. In Romans 13 Paul gives seemingly unqualified statements concerning Christian submission to 'the powers that be', on the grounds that they are appointed by God. For Luther this meant recognizing the authority of princes, so long as they did not oppose the preaching of the gospel. He took their power to make and apply the law as their God-given duty, while placing political authority in a sphere distinct from the rule of the Spirit in the hearts of believers. He thus resisted radical social change (advocated by more extreme wings of the Reformation), and supported the suppression of the Peasants' Revolt. His doctrine of 'two kingdoms' has often led Lutherans to a form of political quietism, with fateful consequences during the Third Reich. Calvin, on the other hand, in different political circumstances proposed a more integrated (though still differentiated) relation between Church and state, and helped shape a 'godly society' in his adopted city, Geneva.

His example inspired other Reformed political experiments (for instance, in Scotland, America and South Africa), in which the interpretation of Romans 13 has played a key part in legitimating a Protestant social order.

The influence of Paul has now rippled through Protestant history for 500 years. Paul's belligerence, amplified by the conflicts of the Reformation, has led to an argumentative spirit within Protestantism, fostering numerous internal fissures; each splinter movement has been inspired by Paul's self-portrait as a lonely warrior for the truth. At the same time, the intensity and flexibility of Protestant theology has forged some of the most ambitious efforts in Western theology to come to terms with the Enlightenment and its aftermath: Ferdinand Christian Baur, Friedrich Schleiermacher, Adolf von Harnack, Karl Barth and Rudolf Bultmann are among the most famous Protestant theologians of the last two centuries, each, in contradictory ways, reactivating core Pauline themes such as Spirit, faith, freedom and grace. At the same time, the Protestant emphasis on the education of ministers, and on the engagement of believers with the Scriptures (in their own mother tongue), has created an intense engagement with Paul in Protestant church life. An abundance of commentaries, lengthy sermons and the discipline of daily, personal Bible study have all been distinctive features of the Protestant tradition, and although the whole of the Bible is theoretically in Protestant view, Paul's letters have undoubtedly enjoyed disproportionate prominence.

The Reformation revolution in church order also directed attention to the material in Paul's letters on church leadership and structure, although the variety of that material has given warrant for different kinds of church. The Pastoral

Epistles have been attractive to those favouring a hierarchy of offices, with overseers (bishops), elders and deacons, but other letters of Paul have inspired rather more fluid forms of leadership. In particular, Paul's instructions on the gifts of the Spirit, including speaking in tongues (1 Corinthians 12—14), have been highly influential within Pentecostal and Charismatic forms of the Protestant tradition. The image of a community where each member has spiritual gifts to share has featured strongly in the characteristically Protestant antipathy to clerical privilege, and its counter-emphasis on 'the priesthood of all believers'.

As we have seen, the Protestant reformers (following Augustine) gave special prominence to Paul's theology of grace, and that theme has shaped Protestant spirituality in profound ways ever since. Protestant believers have been schooled to feel and to express deep personal gratitude for the love of God in Christ, a grace given to unworthy sinners. That gratitude resonates through Protestant liturgies (e.g. the Anglican Prayer Book) and in Protestant church music (from Bach's *Passions* to Charles Wesley's hymns) in ways that continue to engage both emotion and imagination. John Newton's lyric has been popular ever since its composition in 1779: 'Amazing Grace, how sweet the sound, that saved a wretch like me.' That deep Protestant sentiment, founded in a vivid experience of personal change, is modelled on the conversion of Paul and his account of the unconditioned love of God. The capacity of this simple and direct message to cross social hierarchies and ethnic boundaries has been vividly displayed in the Methodist movement and in the deep spirituality and political witness of African Americans. At the same time, the Protestant missionary movements that have fanned out across the globe have been inspired by this Pauline-Protestant expectation of personal conversion. Although contemporary evangelical readings of Paul are, like all readings of his letters, selective in their focus, the explosive growth of evangelical Christianity worldwide is markedly Pauline in its tenor. Enter any evangelical church, within or outside the mainstream denominations, and one is bound to hear Pauline thematics: Christ's atoning death for sin, the free gift of grace, the power of the Spirit, and the love of God 'for me'. Thus, whether on the surface or just beneath it, Paul inhabits the spirituality of hundreds of millions of Christians today.

9

Paul in Jewish–Christian relations

Starting in his lifetime, and right down through history, Paul's relationship to his fellow Jews has been a matter of controversy, but also of deep cultural and political significance. Paul described himself as a 'Jew', and never as a 'Christian'; that term had not been invented in his day. But his letters have been honoured within the Christian Church, which over its first four centuries became increasingly separate from Jewish communities and self-consciously distinct from Judaism. During that period and since, Paul's multiple and mixed comments about Jews and 'Judaism' have played a significant role in the fraught relations between Christians and Jews. The history of European anti-Semitism, and its appalling climax in the Holocaust, form the context for all recent interpretations of Paul and make this topic morally urgent.

There are texts where Paul appears to repudiate his Jewish past, or draws such a sharp contrast between his Jewish upbringing and his present status 'in Christ' that he could be seen, from a later perspective, to adumbrate a clear distinction between 'Judaism' and 'Christianity'. He attributes his former persecution of the Church to his zeal for the Jewish Law (Galatians 1; Philippians 3), and speaks once of his 'former life in Judaism' (Galatians 1.13). Listing his Jewish symbols of value, he declares them worthless in comparison with 'the surpassing worth of knowing Messiah Jesus my Lord'

(Philippians 3.8). He associates the 'present Jerusalem' with slavery and with Ishmael, while those who are free in Christ are considered Abraham's true heirs, like Isaac (Galatians 4.21—5.1). Paul speaks of Jews who 'killed both the Lord Jesus and the prophets' and who displease God by hindering his mission; 'God's wrath', he declares, 'has overtaken them at last' (1 Thessalonians 2.14–16). That comment was written before 70 CE, but it is easy to see how it could be used, in hindsight, to support the widespread early Christian opinion that the Romans' destruction of the Temple, at the end of the Jewish Revolt, was God's definitive judgement on the Jewish nation.

At the same time, there are passages where Paul seems passionately concerned about Jews, and identifies with them as his kinsmen. He lists the privileges of Israelites (Romans 9.1–5) and prays earnestly for their salvation (Romans 10.1). Indeed, in one famous passage he traces the mysterious future of God's mercy, and declares that 'all Israel will be saved' (Romans 11.26) – though that statement has been subject to varied interpretations. Jewish practices like circumcision seem sometimes to be rendered void, sometimes relativized, sometimes affirmed, and sometimes spiritualized as 'the circumcision of the heart' (Romans 2.29). On this, as on other matters, Paul could be 'all things to all people' (1 Corinthians 9.22). As the history of interpretation shows, his legacy is sufficiently ambiguous to be capable of wildly different readings.

Paul's denial that people can be justified by 'works of the law' is a focal instance of this interpretative variety. It was common in the early Church to interpret 'works of the law' as Jewish ritual practices ('ceremonies'), which Paul opposed on the grounds that they had been rendered obsolete since

Christ. Origen (*c*.185–254) and Jerome (*c*.342–420) thus understood Paul's critique to be directed against Jewish sacrifices, Sabbath observance, food laws and circumcision – all regulations of the 'old covenant' that had been superseded by the 'new' (2 Corinthians 3.6). In a Church increasingly distinct from Judaism, though sometimes in competition with it, Paul was read as announcing the end of the Jewish tradition; the destruction of Jerusalem in 70 CE and the failure of the Second Jewish Revolt in 135 CE were taken as confirmation of this reading. In that frame of thought, while the Jewish Scriptures, as the 'Old Testament', were still read in churches, their function was to point forward to Christ. The letter to the Hebrews, often attributed to Paul, was similarly taken to show that the Jewish religion, in the form of Temple sacrifice, had been superseded by the final and perfect sacrifice of Christ.

Augustine, as we have seen, took Paul's polemics to be directed at the 'boasting' that accompanied 'works'; that is, human pride before God (see Chapter 7 above). Luther, recontextualizing Paul's theology in his conflict with the Catholic Church, interpreted 'works of the law' as the good works erroneously thought necessary to merit the favour of God (Chapter 8). As a result, in his polemics against 'our Jews', Luther interpreted Judaism as a form of 'works-righteousness' and self-salvation. After initially hoping that Jews would respond positively to the gospel, once it was properly proclaimed, he became disillusioned, and his late tracts against the Jews (centuries later energetically circulated in the Third Reich) issue shocking appeals for the expulsion of Jews and the destruction of their property. Christian stereotypes of Judaism have many roots, but there can be no doubt that Protestant polemics against

Catholicism, taking inspiration from Luther's reading of Paul, have fuelled caricatures of Judaism as a 'legalistic' religion, both in academic circles and in the popular Christian mind.

The European Enlightenment added a new set of reasons to disparage Judaism, and a new frame in which to interpret Paul. In the early nineteenth century, Ferdinand Christian Baur (1792–1860) celebrated Paul as the key figure in liberating Christianity from the 'shackles' of Judaism: the universal Christian religion had to supersede the particularity represented by Judaism, a national religion. Paul's famous antithesis between 'Spirit' and 'flesh' justified Baur's Hegelian celebration of the Spirit, which rose above the 'fleshly' constrictions of ancestry, ritual and territory. Thus Judaism could be represented as an obstacle to the spiritual progress of European civilization, which for liberal Protestants attained its highest expression in Christian spirituality. The growth of European anti-Semitism had multiple causes, but the interpretation of Paul was an element in some of its theological forms.

In the wake of the Holocaust, a fundamental shift has been required in Christian relations to Jews, and in readings of Paul on Judaism. In the 1960s new historical readings insisted on a clear distinction between Paul's first-century concerns and the issues of the sixteenth-century Reformation. In particular, it was insisted that Paul had not undergone a Protestant-style 'conversion', and had never abandoned his Jewish convictions and hopes. What he described as his 'calling' (Galatians 1.15–16) was not a conversion, but a commission – an apostolic vocation to take the good news to Gentiles. There was thus no fundamental departure from 'Judaism' and no expectation that Jews should change their religion or practice. Paul's hopes for Israel in Romans 9—11 acquired new prominence, as the centre of that letter and not just an appendix, and the fact that Paul's prediction of Israel's salvation is not there expressly linked to faith in Christ led some to insist that there were no grounds for Christian mission to Jews. If Paul, then, was an apostle to Gentiles (only), that left the Jewish covenant unaffected by Christ and Jewish salvation assured in its own 'special way'. Christian dialogue with Jews, and the increasing participation of Jewish scholars in the study of Paul, began to outlaw former caricatures of Judaism, and fostered a rediscovery of a 'Jewish' Paul parallel to the modern insistence that Jesus was a Jew.

One sign of this reaction against older traditions of interpretation is 'the new perspective on Paul', which began with the re-evaluation of ancient Judaism itself. In a landmark book of 1977 (*Paul and Palestinian Judaism*), E. P. Sanders successfully overturned old stereotypes of Judaism, insisting that its concern for obedience to the law is not a matter of 'legalism' or 'works-righteousness', but is framed by the covenant, already granted by God in grace. Sanders traced this 'covenantal nomism' through many Jewish texts contemporary to Paul, challenging the old claim that the Judaism of Paul's day had departed from its biblical, covenantal form. The discovery of the Dead Sea Scrolls (since 1947) had already led to a fresh consideration of ancient Judaism, but Sanders' work strengthened the post-Holocaust mood that was sensitized to any hint of Christian anti-Judaism.

'The new perspective on Paul' (associated especially with James Dunn and N. T. Wright) has dissociated Paul from 'Reformation readings', and grounded Paul's polemics not in a principled opposition to Judaism or a 'works-based' spirituality, but in the historical circumstances of Paul's

Gentile mission. Paul's concerns were first-century and specific: that his Gentile converts did not need to adopt distinctive Jewish practices ('the works of the law'), such as male circumcision, because God had promised to Abraham that *all* the nations of the world would be blessed. In one sense, this constitutes a return to a pre-Augustinian perspective (see above), with the accent lying not on general human tendencies (represented 'typically' in Judaism), but on the historical disputes about the ethnic and cultural characteristics of the early Christian movement. Even so, how these historical disputes are framed intellectually is a matter of acute sensitivity. Was Paul attacking a form of 'nationalistic privilege' and 'ethnocentrism' – or does that way of putting it adopt a distinctively (and dangerously) modern preference for universal sameness over the particularities of difference? Was Paul criticizing only the Gentile adoption of Jewish laws, while leaving his Jewish heritage and his fellow Jews unaffected by the Christ event – or does that way of reading Paul (the 'radical new perspective') clash with the evidence of the letters, overcorrecting a former one-sidedness out of concern for religious tolerance? Or does Paul's relativizing of traditional Jewish categories of worth represent part of his larger recalibration of values, arising from his interpretation of the death and resurrection of Christ as an unconditioned gift? The current swirl of opinion on this matter represents not just divergent readings of Paul, but also conflicting ideologies of religion, and different theological (or anti-theological) construals of what lies at the heart of the Christian tradition.

The debate will continue, not only because of the need for Christianity to purge itself of its long hostility to Judaism but also because Paul's letters contain fuel for many lines of argument. It is possible that the contemporary weight placed on Paul's texts to determine Jewish–Christian relations may be too much for them to bear, and it would certainly reduce the heat in this debate if Paul's comments on this topic, whether acceptable to contemporary ears or not, were simply returned to the first century and left there. But it is inevitable that Christians will continue to turn to Paul for direction on these matters, alongside the equally ambiguous, and equally awkward, Gospel of John; and for as long as they do so, the stakes in the interpretation of Paul will remain high. In our multicultural world, the discussion of 'Paul and Judaism' is to some degree a proxy for the discussion of 'Christianity and other religions' in general, but there will always remain something unique about Christian relations with Judaism, on both historical and theological grounds. Paul remains a controversial voice from the first century, and his scriptural status ensures that he continues to challenge, instruct and upset contemporary readers in our own very different world.

10

Paul as social and cultural critic

Paul's theology is full of stark polarities: power and weakness, wealth and poverty, freedom and slavery. More than that, Paul often deploys these opposites in striking and paradoxical ways: 'whenever I am weak, then I am strong' (2 Corinthians 12.10); 'because he [Christ] was rich, for your sakes he became poor, so that by his poverty you might become rich' (2 Corinthians 8.9); 'though I am free with respect to all, I have made myself a slave to all' (1 Corinthians 9.19). And such paradoxes are not simply wordplay. They represent Paul's ability to scramble the accepted meanings of terms, to invert the normal hierarchies of value, and to view reality from an unusual angle such that new structures of meaning emerge. Where his tradition divided the world into 'Jews' and 'Greeks', 'the circumcised' and 'the uncircumcised', Paul declares, 'neither circumcision is anything nor uncircumcision, but a new creation' (Galatians 6.15). The scope of this new vision can be broad: 'There is neither Jew nor Greek, there is neither slave nor free, there is no male and female; for you are all one in Christ Jesus' (Galatians 3.28). This sounds like a radical challenge to the normal categorizations of Roman society, with their hierarchies of status and value. Reminding his converts in Corinth of their lowly social origins, Paul declares:

> God chose what is foolish in the world to shame the
> wise; God chose what is weak in the world to shame
> the strong; God chose what is low and despised in the
> world, things that are not, to reduce to nothing things that
> are, so that no one might boast in the presence of God.
>
> (1 Corinthians 1.27–29)

That is powerful fuel for a new, even revolutionary view of the social order.

In recent centuries, this radical streak in Paul's theology has attracted (or repelled) those seeking to reimagine and reframe their cultural heritage. Friedrich Nietzsche (1844–1900) accused Paul of corrupting the teaching of Jesus, inventing Christianity as a religion of resentment and hate, with a 'slave morality' that sided with the weak against all that is 'noble'. Karl Barth (1886–1968), on the other hand, found in Paul's theology, and especially in his letter to the Romans, the essential antidote to the false European pride that had celebrated its 'religion' and 'ethics' as the highest achievements of civilization, while giving its liberal endorsement to the First World War. For Barth, what Paul grasped first and foremost was the 'infinite qualitative difference' between God and humanity, such that no human achievements or powers can reach across the gulf – only the grace of God which both exposes that gulf and bridges it. Thus Paul's critique of human power and pride is based not on a social or political agenda, but on a theological recognition of the 'God-ness' of God. Nonetheless, Barth's leading role in the 'Confessing Church', which refused to offer allegiance to Hitler, indicated how his theology had significant political effects.

More recently, a number of European philosophers (Jacob Taubes, Giorgio Agamben, Slavoj Žižek, Stanislas Breton and Alain Badiou) have 'rediscovered' Paul as a thinker who can enable us to imagine possibilities beyond the political and cultural cul-de-sacs of the contemporary Western world. Badiou (b.1937), for instance, while distancing himself from Paul's religious beliefs, acclaims Paul as a seminal figure in the way he configures truth as founded in an unconditioned *event* (for Paul, the grace of God in the event of Christ). Out of this event arises a kind of 'universalism' that is not the false universalism of global capitalism but is also unconfined by cultural particularity and the divisive effects of identity politics. Badiou thus offers a 'secularized' version of Paul's theology of grace, but recognizes in it a force that traverses, without erasing, social and cultural differences. For Badiou the truth declared by those who are reconstituted by the event neither affirms nor rejects their cultural and social particularities: it crosses them 'at a diagonal'. The radical potential of Paul, on this reading, resides not so much in a new bounded community that transfers people from one social condition to another, but in the capacity to 'sit loose' to all social and cultural conditions, with unpredictable results.

As much as he can excite some, Paul can also disappoint those looking for a radical social vision, and the disappointment typically arises from an anachronistic expectation that he will speak in modern, liberal terms. The textbook example of this potential misfit between Paul and modernity is the question of slavery, on which Paul's letters were invoked extensively on *both* sides of the eighteenth- and nineteenth-century debates. On the one hand, defenders of slavery cited the household codes in the Pauline letters, where slaves are instructed to obey their masters in everything, out of fear for the Master, Jesus (Colossians 3.20–25).

Slave-owners were therefore fond of Paul, and frequently cited his letter to Philemon, where the slave Onesimus, even though he had become a Christian, was sent back by Paul to his owner. This same letter was also cited by some opponents of slavery since, on sending him back, Paul described Onesimus as 'no longer as a slave, but more than a slave, a beloved brother' (Philemon 16). That phrase, in invoking the category 'brother', could help recategorize slaves in Enlightenment terms as fellow humans – 'brothers' and 'sisters' with claims to human dignity and human rights. What became clear in this long and complex debate is that Paul could not be cited unequivocally as favouring the emancipation of slaves; while he relativized the status of slave and free (1 Corinthians 7.17–24), he did not view all forms of slavery as unequivocally evil, as we have come to do. It has been tempting, in hindsight, to impute to him our own social perspective, and to excuse his silence on slave emancipation as a matter of political pragmatism: if he had declared his true view, he would have endangered the fledgling Christian movement. From that perspective, he 'sowed the seeds' that would eventually flower 1,800 years later. But it is probably more honest to say that Paul did not view legal freedom as an absolute good, but as beneficial only if it enabled fuller service to Christ. At the same time, he undercut the significance normally given to social hierarchies in a way that has the capacity to destabilize social differences, without necessarily eradicating them.

The same problematics have arisen in relation to gender and to sexuality; in both cases, Paul seems radical in certain respects, but not 'progressive' in modern terms. With regard to gender, the same household codes that enjoin slaves to obey their masters instruct wives to obey their husbands (Colossians 3.18; Ephesians 5.21–33). Moreover, in 1 Timothy Paul's authority stands behind a statement that requires women to be silent and refuses them permission to teach (1 Timothy 2.8–15). In the modern era, with its critical distinction between 'authentic' and 'deutero-Pauline' letters, these letters have been distanced from 'the original Paul' in academic circles, but their attribution to Paul and their canonical status ensure that they are still cited by the majority of Christians for the proper ordering of gender relations. Elsewhere the picture is more complex. Phoebe, Prisca and other female figures are highlighted by Paul as taking prominent positions in church leadership (Romans 16), and Junia is even described as 'prominent among the apostles' (Romans 16.7) – although many translations have wrongly taken her to be a man called Junias. In Paul's most contorted passage on gender, women are distinguished from men on the grounds of Genesis 2—3, in a 'natural' hierarchy used to justify female head-covering (1 Corinthians 11.2–16). Here and elsewhere Paul seems to assume the standard ancient subordination of women to men. That reading has, of course, suited most Christian interpreters down through history, and still suits some today.

In recent times, more radical potential has been found in Paul's honouring of women in leadership and in the statement from Galatians 3.28, cited above: 'there is no male and female' (often wrongly translated, 'there is neither male nor female'). This has been taken to represent a kind of gender blindness that relativizes gender difference, but the statement has also been read in a rather different sense, as undercutting the high value traditionally placed on marriage (it appears to echo, and contradict, 'male and female he created them', Genesis 1.27). Certainly, the most radical things Paul says about gender are to be found in a judgement unattractive to the modern world: in 1 Corinthians 7 he values celibacy over marriage, because the unattached person (male or female) is better able to give undistracted attention to the concerns of Christ. Here again, Paul's theology shows its capacity to scramble our taken-for-granted assumptions about sexuality and gender, though it does so from an angle that fits neither conservative 'family values' nor the liberal desire for sexual freedom and individual autonomy.

There can be no denying that Paul's legacy has most frequently been utilized for traditional mores and conservative causes. In the current disputes about homosexuality, Paul's statements in Romans 1.26–27 are the key evidence for the conservative Christian ethic, though their precise meaning and their place within his wider theology are heavily contested. In political terms, his seemingly blanket statements in Romans 13 have generally encouraged submission to state authority: 'Let every person be subject to the governing authorities; for there is no authority except from God' (Romans 13.1). That text has certainly inhibited resistance even to such oppressive regimes as the Third Reich and the apartheid regime in South Africa. In current 'post-colonial' readings of Paul, the more socially subversive dimensions of his thought have been given greater prominence, and his expectation of believers' ultimate allegiance to Christ has suggested to some that there is a 'hidden transcript' in his letters, which proclaim 'Jesus is Lord' in order to whisper 'and Caesar is not'. In all such judgements, of course, there is a danger of wishful thinking, a desire to have Paul articulate what our current political agenda would like him to think and say.

Such examples illustrate a basic rule of hermeneutics: texts do not simply 'speak' (as in the frequently voiced claim, 'the Bible says . . .'). Rather, texts (even biblical texts) are *given* voice and influence by *human interpreters*, who inevitably select, prioritize and construe them according to their own social locations and their cultural or political agendas. That places an onus of responsibility on the interpreter, who cannot claim to be simply 'repeating' what Paul says. And this responsibility is all the more difficult, and significant, in the case of such polyvalent texts as the letters of Paul. Even individual letters of Paul can be heard to pull in more than one direction on social and political matters, and once one puts together all 13 letters attributed to Paul (not to mention their larger canonical context), the ambiguity of these texts is increased still further, and the space expanded for the creative work of the interpreter. In the ongoing tussles over the legacy of Paul, it would serve us well to recognize this hermeneutical activity, in which we are committed both to reading his letters carefully and to *making* responsible sense of them in our own contemporary context. And it might also serve us well to recognize in Paul a figure who, for better or worse, does not fit our political categories of 'conservative' or 'liberal'. He has, we may judge, his own strengths and limitations, but he does not fit what *we* expect with regard to such values as liberty, equality and tolerance. Moreover, his theological perspective is apt to undercut the supreme importance that we accord to such matters as ethnicity, wealth, gender and status, but with ambiguous effect. Relativizing all such identities under the supreme and only good of belonging to Christ could result in leaving the status quo intact, devoid of ultimate significance and therefore untouched. As history has shown, that can lead to appalling injustices, the demeaning of women, the dehumanization of slaves and discrimination against whole racial groups. Alternatively, the subversive effects of grace, which operates without regard to prior 'worth' but accords new value and identity as given by God, can loosen the structures of tradition and hierarchy. That can enable social experiments like Paul's own innovative communities, which crossed social boundaries and reconfigured allegiances and obligations. As history also has shown, this can lead to an equalizing social momentum, an escape from regnant stereotypes and a political independence of mind that resists the totalizing claims of nation, race or state. Perhaps it is precisely Paul's misfit with our normal agendas that makes him still useful as an irritant to our social and political discourse.

Paul, as we saw in Chapter 1, has been a controversial figure from the very beginning, and controversy, in evaluation of his worth and in the interpretation of his letters, continues to this day. But it is better to be controversial than forgotten. As the Western world loses touch with its Christian heritage, it is likely that Paul will become an increasingly unfamiliar figure. For those unsympathetic to his theological convictions, he will appear an aggressive, authoritative figure of the distant past, with unreconstructed attitudes out of tune with modern agendas. At the same time, he remains an inescapable part of the Western cultural heritage, ever available as a gadfly, who has the annoying, but fascinating, habit of seeing the world from an unusual perspective. And where the Church remains and even grows (as currently in the non-Western world), Paul's influence is bound to continue in his canonical guise. At a popular level, the sheer difficulty of Paul's letters (their argumentative complexity and historical opaqueness) may limit their influence beyond those 'purple passages' (like the description of love in 1 Corinthians 13) that communicate immediately across the centuries. But as long as Christian theology remains in dialogue with its biblical canon, it will endeavour to explain and mediate Paul's message to each new generation and in every cultural context. For this purpose, Paul's rhetorical and cultural flexibility, and the ambiguities these create, may prove more a blessing than a curse: his texts are sufficiently 'open' to spawn creative translations and fresh interpretations in the unpredictable conditions of the future. And because his message is self-described as 'good news', interpreters will be bound to bring out, in ever fresh ways, its creative, liberating, saving and life-transforming potential.

Further reading

Allen, Michael and Linebaugh, Jonathan (eds), *Reformation Readings of Paul* (Downers Grove, IL: IVP Academic, 2015).

Badiou, Alain, *Saint Paul: The Foundation of Universalism* (Stanford, CT: Stanford University Press, 2003).

Barclay, John M. G., *Paul and the Gift* (Grand Rapids, MI: Eerdmans, 2015).

Dunn, James D. G. (ed.), *The Cambridge Companion to St Paul* (Cambridge: Cambridge University Press, 2003).

Gaventa, Beverly R., *When in Romans: An Invitation to Linger with the Apostle Paul* (Grand Rapids, MI: Baker Academic, 2016).

Hays, Richard B., *Echoes of Scripture in the Letters of Paul* (New Haven, CT: Yale University Press, 1989).

Harrill, J. Albert, *Paul the Apostle: His Life and Legacy in Their Roman Context* (New York: Cambridge University Press, 2012).

Hooker, Morna D., *Paul: A Short Introduction* (Oxford: Oneworld, 2003).

Horrell, David G., *An Introduction to the Study of Paul*, 3rd edition (London: T & T Clark, 2015).

Meeks, Wayne A., *The First Urban Christians: The Social World of the Apostle Paul* (New Haven, CT: Yale University Press, 1983).

Reasoner, Mark, *Romans in Full Circle: A History of Interpretation* (Louisville, KY: Westminster John Knox, 2005).

Riches, John, *Galatians Through the Centuries*, Blackwell Bible Commentaries (Oxford: Blackwell, 2008).

Sanders, E. P., *Paul: The Apostle's Life, Letters, and Thought* (Minneapolis, MN: Fortress Press, 2015).

Westerholm, Stephen, *Perspectives Old and New on Paul: The 'Lutheran' Paul and his Critics* (Grand Rapids, MI: Eerdmans, 2004).

Westerholm, Stephen (ed.), *The Blackwell Companion to Paul* (Chichester: Wiley-Blackwell, 2011).

Wright, N. T., *Paul: Fresh Perspectives* (London: SPCK, 2005).

Index

1 Corinthians 19, 39
1 Peter 35
1 Thessalonians 7, 18–19
1 Timothy 16, 41
2 Corinthians 19–20, 39
2 Peter 49, 51
2 Thessalonians 16, 41
2 Timothy 17, 41

Abraham 11, 23–4, 28, 73, 77
Acts of Paul and Thecla, The 34, 41–2
Acts of the Apostles 4, 8, 10, 33, 39–40
Adam 23, 52, 57, 59
Agamben, Giorgio 80
Apollos 11, 39
Aquinas, Thomas 62–3
Anselm 62
anti-Semitism 72, 74–5, 77
atonement 62, 71
    see also expiation
Augustine 54, 56–63, 74

Bach, Johann Sebastian 70
Badiou, Alain 81
baptism 6, 21, 35
Barnabas 9
Barth, Karl 69, 80
Baur, Ferdinand Christian 69, 75

Breton, Stanislas 80
Bultmann, Rudolf 69

Calvin, John 67–8
canon 14, 51
celibacy 34, 41–2, 62, 66, 83–4
Chrysostom, John 54, 56
church structure 69–70
churches of Paul 30–7
circumcision
    as Jewish practice 5, 36, 58, 74, 77
    in Paul's letters 26–7, 73, 79
Clement of Rome 15
Colossians, letter to the 16, 67
covenant 64, 74, 76
creation, new 27, 28, 43, 79

Dunn, James 76

election 60–1, 68
Ephesians, letter to the 16, 41, 67
Erastus 30
expiation 54

faith in Christ 57, 65, 69, 76
family 31, 33–4
    see also marriage

Index

food
  in Jewish law 26, 33–4, 36, 58, 74
  in Paul 26
freedom 73, 79

Galatians, letter to the 15, 20, 38, 43, 65
gender 82–4
Gentiles, Paul's mission to 3, 7, 11, 24, 28–9, 76–7
God, oneness of 23, 25–7
grace/gift
  in Augustine 58–61
  in Barth 80
  in Judaism 28, 76
  in Luther 64–7
  in Paul 7–8, 21, 28, 39, 77, 81, 86
  in Protestantism 70–1
  see also mercy

Harnack, Adolf von 69
Hebrews, letter to the 4–5, 74
hermeneutics 85
homosexuality 84

idolatry 19, 23, 26, 32–6
Ignatius of Antioch 15
interpretation 54–5, 63
  see also hermeneutics
Irenaeus 44
Israel 12
  in Calvin 67
  in Paul 21, 24, 27–9, 52, 73, 76

James 15, 38
Jerome 57, 74
Jerusalem 5, 10, 25, 33, 34, 74
  and Paul 6, 9–10, 21, 33, 38, 44, 73
  see also Temple
Jesus
  crucifixion and death 8, 21
  and God 27
  as Messiah 5, 24
  resurrection 5, 7–8, 21, 28
Judaism 33–4
  and Christianity 11–12, 29, 72–8
  and Paul 3, 6–8, 11–12, 23–9, 72–3
  see also Israel
Junia 83
justification 21, 53, 65–7

Law/Torah 5–6, 14, 20, 25, 29, 38, 49, 50, 72
  see also works of the law
Lombard, Peter 62
Luther, Martin 64–8, 74

Marcion 42–4
marriage 31, 34–5, 41, 66, 83–4
  see also celibacy
Martyrdom of Paul, The 42
mercy 21, 24, 28–9, 61, 73

Newton, John 70
Nietzsche, Friedrich 80

Index

Onesimus 15, 20, 35, 82
Origen 74

participation in Christ 54
Pastoral letters 16–17, 41, 69–70
Paul
  authorship questions 5, 15–18, 83
  calling/conversion 7–8, 27, 39, 70, 75
  Catholic reception 51, 59
  citizenship 33
  collection of money for Jerusalem 9–10
  death 11, 37, 40, 42
  expectation of the end 9, 19, 28, 52
  letters 4–5, 13–22
  life 6–11
  new perspective on 76–7
  as Pharisee 6
  Protestant reception 51, 64–71
  sources for 4–5
  as theologian 13–14, 62–3
  see also individual letters
Pelagius 60
Peter 9, 16, 38, 65
  see also 1 Peter; 2 Peter
political authorities 37, 68–9, 84
Philemon, letter to 15, 20, 22, 35, 82
Philippians, letter to the 21
Phoebe 15, 83

predestination 60–1
Prisca 83

Roman Empire 32–3, 37, 42–3
Romans, letter to the 13, 15, 21–2, 59, 67

Sabbath 26, 34, 36, 58, 74
sanctification 67–8
Sanders, E. P. 76
Schleiermacher, Friedrich 69
Scripture
  Jewish/Old Testament 6, 8, 11–12, 23, 26, 28, 52
  Paul as 49–55
Silvanus/Silas 9
sin 21, 53, 57–9
slavery 20, 31, 35–56, 79, 81–2
Spirit 6, 20, 21, 54, 60, 68–71, 75
  spiritual body 44, 50

Taubes, Jacob 80
Temple, in Jerusalem 25, 33, 34, 73, 74
Tertullian 44
Third Reich 68, 74, 80, 84
Timothy 9, 16–17
  see also 1 Timothy; 2 Timothy
Titus 9, 16
Titus, letter to 16, 41

universalism 75, 77, 81

Valentinus 44

Index

Weber, Max 68

Wesley, Charles 70

works of the law 57–8, 65, 73–5

Wright, N. T. 76

Žižek, Slavoj 80